The Challenge
of
Achievement

The Challenge
of
Achievement

*Helping
Your Child Succeed*

Shirley Gould

HAWTHORN BOOKS, INC.
Publishers / NEW YORK
A Howard & Wyndham Company

To the achievers: Ruth, Arthur, Shepard—evidence of my life

Contents

The Challenge
of
Achievement

1
Introduction

Success may no longer be the prime goddess of our society; but it is certainly the cherished dream of all parents that the children they bring into the world achieve success among their fellow human beings. Those people who raise children that are not their biological heirs—adoptive parents, foster parents, and guardians—are just as eager for their youngsters to thrive and reach success. We all want full lives for our children, not only in terms of material wealth, but also in terms of satisfying human relationships. We want them to have it all: worldly goods, loving intimates, and the respect and admiration of other people.

Often we want for our children the very attributes we ourselves miss, and the more conscientious we are the more painful it is to watch our children flounder. Then we put more pressure on them, trying to guarantee that they will enjoy better lives than we have. That very pressure often works to the opposite purpose, pushing them down and making life harder for them and for us.

Because we're human, we make many mistakes in our lives and in bringing up our children. But because we're intelligent human beings, we can learn to minimize those mistakes. Sometimes we observe that the very words and actions we use in attempting to help our children succeed have the opposite effect, and we remain bewildered.

Naturally, the success of each individual is largely a result of that person's innate abilities, effort, and determination, to say nothing of the "breaks"—luck. But within those limits, as parents we have great opportunities to help our children reach their full potential. The earlier one starts, the better; but it's never too late. You can change your attitude toward your children and your communication and activities with them so that you can be more helpful in their attempts to move out into the world.

The topic of this book is "How to help your children reach their full potential," which is a cumbersome way of saying that I want to help parents of preteenagers be effective partners with their offspring, enhancing children's abilities and opportunities as much as possible. For children to achieve, they need a combination of self-confidence, self-esteem, and self-respect: in short, a sense of personal worth. With a strong sense of personal worth, each experience contributes to learning and growth and leads to additional achievement.

Many studies conducted by educators show that a child's self-esteem is closely tied to that child's achievement. If self-esteem is low, so is performance. Educators have developed many ways to measure achievement and self-confidence and the indications are consistent that the person with good solid self-esteem is best equipped to do well. What the many studies prove is that those children with a high sense of their own personal value perform better on the many tests that have been devised to measure achievement. But what the studies don't cover is how the children first obtain that confidence in their own worth. They don't shed much light for parents who want to help their children achieve.

You may think of famous people who have achieved success in spite of deep feelings of personal inferiority and at the cost of personal relationships. We hear about them all the time. They are the ones who claim that success cost them their marriages, or their family lives, or that success came only after heartbreak. It may seem that these people acquired their fame despite feelings of inferiority, disproving my statements. In fact, they were probably working to overcome such feelings. No one knows what the course of a life might have been; we can only see what happened. When children are small, with life ahead of them, the adults around them have the best opportunity to help them toward fulfillment and accomplishment.

The really successful person is the one who achieves in the usual sense and also makes satisfying personal relationships. It is not necessary to give up one in order to have the other, to choose between success and satisfaction.

Regardless of the research that shows the importance of personal worth to achievement, there is very little information for parents who want to know how to go about helping their children to gain it. How do you teach them to have a sense of worth, to make a decision and trust it, to live in harmony with others? It isn't easy but it's possible and no one needs advanced degrees to do it. The best intentions and the most effort will not necessarily result in successful offspring, but an encouraging attitude, informed effort, and specific kinds of communication can make it happen.

What it takes is a combination of many things: trust in and respect for your child, faith in the future, and the ability to believe that the young person has an innate capacity to be an achiever. Above all, of course, is your absolute conviction of the child's value as a person.

It isn't necessary to focus all your efforts on one child, either. Many times parents do this, especially on their firstborn, when parenthood is new and exciting. Each child in the family can profit from the kinds of relationships and parenting techniques you will find in this book. And in the process, you the parent may find more success for yourself too.

When I say "parent" I mean any adult who has a close relationship with a child, and when I say "child" I mean a young person from birth until about the time of adolescence. After the onset of puberty, as a youngster becomes exposed to more and more outside influences, opportunities to exert your own influence diminish.

This is not a book about problems with children. If you're having behavior problems in your family, you won't find the answers here. Another thing you won't find is a tribute to material achievement. My concept of a successful person is not the one who has accumulated the most. It is, instead, a book about personal achievement.

Here you will find guidance in the three strands of development that braid together as children grow toward the full use of their abilities. These three strands consist of:

1. Skills and knowledge
2. Self-esteem and self-confidence
3. Life's values

They are similar to but not quite the same as the three tasks of life mentioned by Alfred Adler* and identified by Rudolf Dreikurs and Harold Mosak:**

1. Work
2. Love
3. Friendship

The child's work is to acquire skills and knowledge and to learn personal responsibility. The task of love for a child is to love parents, siblings, relatives, friends, and self and to understand the duties that love imposes. The third task, usually translated from the German *Gemeinschaftsgefühl* as "social interest," is concern for others, the ability to participate, and the willingness to contribute to the common good. In order to express it, a person must be firmly grounded in human values and understand the impact of human relationships.

---

* Alfred Adler was the eminent social psychologist whose theories of democratic living form the foundation for the ideas in this book.

** Rudolf Dreikurs and Harold H. Mosak, "The Tasks of Life: Adler's Three Tasks," *The Individual Psychologist* (1969), Vol. 4, no. 1, pp. 18–22.

2
Definitions

Several key words describe the subject matter covered in this book. Because our language is deficient in describing what we all want for our children, definitions of those key words will help to illuminate the basic ideas. All parents yearn and hope for their children. Sometimes their ideas are vague; sometimes they are spoken. We all assume that everyone wants the same things and that everyone else knows what we think, but in reality we have many different priorities. To some parents it is most important that their children make a lot of money; to others fame comes first; and still others long for higher social standing for their offspring. Often the wishes that are spoken don't match the ones that are unspoken.

Many parents say, "I only want my child to be happy." We can't describe what happiness is, or what makes it. Inside, where we feel vulnerable, a parent may be thinking, "I hope she gets more out of life than I have," or "I hope he won't make the same mistakes I did." Or happiness may mean to a parent, "My child's happiness will make up for my own unhappiness."

Regardless of how it's expressed, parents want their children to rise, to gain, to "make it." The words *achieve*, *achievement*, *succeed*, and *success* all symbolize those wishes, and they will be defined. The word *potential* is another that is frequently used in connection with children's achievement. Both the dictionary meanings and the meanings in common usage for all these words follow.

What Is Achievement?

Webster's Third New International Dictionary has several meanings for the word *achieve*. Two of them are: (1) "to bring to a successful conclusion; to carry out successfully"; and (2) "to get as the result of exertion; succeed in obtaining or gaining." It also says it means "to attain a desired end or aim; reach a certain level of performance." The example used to explain this meaning is significant. It cites "pupils who fail to achieve after promotion." This calls our attention to the fact that pupils are continually being watched and measured in terms of whether or not they achieve. It seems typical that the example mentions failure to achieve rather than success in achieving. Emphasis is on inability rather than on ability.

In the definition of the word *achievement* there is an elaboration of the idea of the struggle to achieve, the actual movement necessary toward progress. Besides "the act of achieving" it calls achievement "successful completion" and "a result brought about by resolve, persistence, or endeavor." In this last sense we are reminded that it takes more than talent to be an achiever. One needs to be able to figure out other paths to the goal when the obvious one seems blocked and also to stick to a task until it is completed. There's an old cliche that genius is "ten percent inspiration and ninety percent perspiration," also pointing out that without perseverance there isn't much achievement. Perseverance is a quality that can be learned, unlike talent, which is innate. There isn't any magic in learning to keep on working. A person's attitude makes the difference between the wish to quit and the ability to sustain.

The place of achievement in the life of a student is noted in *Webster's* in another definition of achievement that calls it "performance by a student in a course; quality and quantity of a student's work during a given period." It's interesting that even dictionary compilers assume that achievement is most concentrated in the school.

In the common, everyday sense of the words *achieve* and *achievement*, we understand them to mean the measure of a child's progress. In order to grow from a child to an adult, it is necessary that the person expand not only in terms of physical growth but in emotional development and mental competence. This expansion happens in very small steps. Often we lose sight of such small steady gains in our zeal to find big noticeable ones that we can brag about.

Potential is a very loaded word. It wasn't heard much until the language of the teachers' colleges became familiar to parents. Anyone who has a child in grade school is now accustomed to hearing "He's not living up to his full potential" or "Her potential is limited." Either expression can make a mother or father feel awful, and judging by the frequency with which those statements are made a lot of parents must feel downhearted.

Limitations

It is significant that one does not hear, "This child has progressed beyond her potential," or "We don't know what his potential might be." The concept of the limits of potential is part of the philosophy of calling attention to a person's mistakes and limits rather than emphasizing a person's strengths. In the old-fashioned school we were graded on the basis of 100, meaning 100 percent correct answers. Our spelling papers, our arithmetic problems, our other tests—all were calculated on the basis of how many we had wrong. In the modern school there are more sophisticated ways of marking grades, but most emphasis is still on what a child does wrong. Our society is permeated with the idea that no one needs to be informed when he or she is correct or does something well, but everyone needs to be corrected, even reprimanded, for making a mistake or having a knowledge gap.

We regard potential as some kind of fixed limit, but it isn't. We often act as if it were a noun, naming an object or a concept. But it is also an adjective that needs other words to make it a complete thought. *Webster's* defines *potential* as "existing in possibility for changing or developing in a state of actuality," and the *Random House Dictionary* defines the word as "possible, as opposed to actual; capable of being or becoming; a latent excellence or ability that may or may not be developed."

In common usage, we speak of a person's potential in the sense of the last definition: a latent ability that may or may not be developed. No one can know what a child's actual potential is unless the child is permanently and visibly handicapped, in which case we know what certain of his or her limitations are. Even the handicapped child needs assistance to develop potential in ways that are not limited. For this child it may be crucial to emphasize qualities of wholeness rather than the boundaries of possibility that the handicap imposes.

It is a disservice to any person, especially a child, to set up a "potential" and then to judge that person according to whether he or she has yet attained that mark. It is as if we were to decide at birth how tall a child is to grow, set a mark on the wall, and then measure if the youngster meets the mark. As far as I know, parents do not do that; yet they set up other expectations of performance to determine whether their children measure up to them. Expectations do not do harm by themselves. It is how we as parents act if they are not met that has a poor effect on our children. The next time you feel disappointed in your child, consider whether your feeling is like the one you might have if the child didn't reach six feet in height.

None of us knows our own potential, for over every human being is the specter of uncertainty. None of us knows what we may be capable of; each of us knows the wonder of coping well with a situation we did not expect. The ultimate uncertainty is that none of us even knows how many days we have to live. As long as we live we are, in the words of the definition of potential, "capable of being or becoming."

Not long ago, at a university commencement, an acquaintance had just been cited for honors in her chosen field and was still glowing from the satisfaction of completion. As she clutched her degree, I overheard her say to her family, "I wish I could find the college counselor I went to see when I was nineteen. I was having trouble with my studies and wanted help. It was tough to be away from home and on my own for the first time, and I was afraid I couldn't keep up with the work. He said, 'You're doing as well as can be expected within your limitations. I checked your test scores and you're just average or a little below.' I felt so bad I dropped out and got married. At least I could excel at cooking, cleaning, and having children, and that's where I put all my effort. I didn't think about a college education until twenty years later when my oldest son was a freshman. Now I'd like to show that counselor this diploma with honors and see what he'd say about my limitations!"

Of course the schools need to measure children's aptitudes and abilities. They have to put them in categories, to organize classes, or there would be chaos. When all the children were taught in one-room schoolhouses, an individual child could learn at his or her own pace. My mother, an immigrant to the United States at age twelve, told of the school across the road from her father's farm. In that one room with one teacher she studied reading and spelling at the first-grade level because the language was new to her; but in arithmetic she was with the eighth graders because the concepts of mathematics were familiar to her and she handled them well.

In the modern school the grades are keyed to chronological age. A child enters the primary school at about the age of six and is expected to move through it one year at a time in company with classmates. If they don't learn what they're supposed to when the allotted time has passed, one or many are judged deficient.

We can't go back to the one-room school; that would not solve our problems. Our educational system has produced more good than harm; it has produced tests and measurements, scores and grades, all to measure what the pupils are learning. We must be careful not to worship the techniques. There are fast tracks and slow tracks for the bright ones and the poor learners. Such segregation may help organize schools and classrooms and lead to valuable educational opportunities for the children, but damage is done when children are labeled. It makes no difference if the labels are blue birds and red birds rather than fast and slow. The children catch on quickly to the distinctions and they know which classmates measure up and which do not. If the potential of a slow child is judged to be limited, the teacher may abandon efforts to teach, justifying this act on the basis that it would be a waste of time to try to reach Jenny's ability since her potential is so limited.

Even when a child does reach an advanced level, we still don't know if her or his potential is reached, because it's possible that the child may move on to greater success. The concept of the "late bloomer" was invented to account for those people who seemed to have limited potential, but later proved that the ability was there all the time, merely needing the appropriate opportunity to be developed, or possibly the appropriate stimulus. The graduate whom I overheard probably would be called a "late bloomer," but who knows how much sooner she might have blossomed had her counselor been more optimistic about her chances. She might have been a better, happier mother, besides, had she not felt defeated as a student. We don't know what greater achievements any late bloomer might have attained if the environment for growth had been more favorable at an earlier time.

Success has as many definitions as there are individuals who think about it. *Webster's* says it's "the degree or measure of attaining a desired end; a succeeding fully or in accordance with one's desires" or, more pertinent to our topic, "the attainment of wealth, position, esteem, favor, or eminence." *Random House* says success is "the favorable or prosperous termination of attempts or endeavors" or "the attainment of wealth, position, honors, or the like." Defining *succeed* one need only think of those actions that lead to success. Synonyms for succeed are "flourish, prosper, and thrive."

However it is defined or expressed, each of us wants for our children the conditions in which they will flourish, prosper, and thrive. We want to help them learn how to function in the world so that they themselves will feel successful. It is more valuable to feel successful by yourself and for yourself than it is to win success in the eyes of the world, for it is our own selves that we must all live with for the rest of our lives. One can only reach success by one's own inner standards, and when we believe in our own value we are then equipped to gain success among our fellowmen.

If you are a parent, you will find as you read that the suggestions made are within your sphere. All of them are available to you, and you can select the ways in which you feel most able to help your child, adding others as you learn. If you are not a parent but have other contact with a child or children, you will need to choose more carefully among the proposals. Whatever your connection, you will find you can contribute to the child's own sense of value and to the ultimate success of his or her efforts.

Parental Pressure

Even though it's true that you can be a powerful force in your children's success, it is just as true that if they do not reach success you have not failed. Much of the pressure exerted on children to succeed comes from adults' wishes to impress others by showing off their offspring. Especially adults who feel less than worthy have a tendency to want to prove their value through their children.

Whether they have beauty, talent, brains, or seem unendowed, it is the children's work to develop themselves, and it is to their honor when success comes. We must not forget that whatever the ties that bind us to one another, each of us (including all the children) is a separate individual with a separate set of motives and capacities.

Forgetting this, parents often push their children in a direction that is self-serving. Then if the children succeed the parents take the credit; if they fail the parents take the blame. The destructive pressures that parents often place on their children in an effort to push them toward achievement are often a result of the parents' misguided attempts to make up for what they perceive as their own failings. The worst of it is that the more pressure a parent exerts the less the offspring actually prospers.

The first idea you must accept if you're going to help your child be a success is that the child is a separate individual, able to make decisions at a very early age. He or she can thwart your best intentions, rebel against your kindest motives, fight your values, and defeat your efforts. On the other hand, in your close relationships with the child you have many opportunities to assist in his or her development. If you can learn to create harmony in addition to the love you hold for one another, you will then have an atmosphere conducive to mutual trust and respect so that the child can profit from your efforts and you can have the satisfaction of watching your youngster's abilities and talents develop.

In his famous *Paradise Lost* John Milton said, "The childhood shows the man as morning shows the day." Later, William Wordsworth, in the poem "My Heart Leaps Up When I Behold," said, "The child is father of the man." This is a phrase we've all heard and repeated, but it's worth reminding ourselves that the adult is already within each child. All the potential capabilities for success are there. Growing up is a process in which the environment, the events, and the people around help to shape a person. But it is the person, the individual, who perceives herself or himself, the world all about, and decides what sense to make of it. It is a succession of individual experiences, decisions, and perceptions that determines what kind of an adult each child will become and whether success will adorn that life.

3

The Adlerian Approach to Life

Regardless of the age of your child, as you read this you still have an opportunity to help in a way that will make achievement more likely. To be practical it is necessary to examine what the child has to do now and in the future.

As we live, we fashion the braid (as described in chapter 1) made up of three strands: work, love, and friendship. As in a braid, no one strand is more important than another, nor is one bigger than another. All three strands combine to make a broader, stronger cord. In fact, in his early writings, Adler made such a comparison. He spoke of the "three main ties" of life. Ties may be thought of as strands, cords, ribbons, or similar connecting fasteners.

Adler emphasized that each person can live only in a society composed of other human beings. He was the first to notice and declare that persons interact with other people in their development and in their daily lives. He showed us that no one is alone but each of us is embedded in the company of other human beings. Adler spoke of the ties that bind us, saying "every human being is bound by definite ties; his development takes place within a definite framework and he must conform his decisions to this framework. These three main ties are set by the facts that we are living in one particular place in the universe and must develop within the limits and possibilities that our circumstances set for us; that we are living among others of our own kind to whom we must learn to adapt ourselves; and that we are living in two sexes with the future of our race dependent on the relations of these two sexes."*

The "ties" of which Adler wrote early in his career he also called "problems" and "questions." Others who followed his reasoning spoke of "demands," and generally we now consider them as "tasks." When we speak of the tasks, we ask the question, "For what purpose are we here?" and, as we consider our roles in relation to our children, we ask, "For what does this child need to be prepared?"

In order to meet the tasks of life, a child needs to develop (as described in chapter 1) skills and knowledge (the child's work); self-esteem and self-confidence (the child's perception of self); and a value system (the child's relation to others and the universe). These form the basis of the child's individual approach to the adult life tasks.

All our perceptions of life can be seen as aspects of the tasks of life. Remembering that the three named are roughly equal, we can examine them individually. The order in which they appear has no significance.

Work

Occupation, or work, is what one does to ensure survival on the earth. In order to continue to exist, every

* Alfred Adler, *What Life Should Mean to You*, p. 264.

person needs a supply of the basic necessities of life. In our society, where aristocracy has been mostly eliminated, it is assumed that everyone is responsible for himself or herself. Children and infirm or disabled people are dependent upon others. Supporting persons are required to furnish sustenance not only for themselves, but for their dependents as well. Sometimes this support comes from parents in a family; other times from the community, or some combination of both. Since we have also eliminated child labor, children are cared for by others and spend their childhood getting ready to become independent.

It is the need for adult independence that ought to shape a child's learning. Adults often forget that children are in a constant state of growth and development. Young people need continual expansion in their opportunities for individual independence in order to learn how to handle increasing responsibilities. Every day of their lives, children need to do things for themselves, to make their own decisions, and also to make mistakes. Only through such experiences does a young person learn to grow. A good rule for a parent to follow is "Never do anything for a child that he or she can do for himself or herself."

Sometimes you can't be sure what a child is capable of. It seems much easier to continue to give service, to be the competent adult who can do the job better and faster. Then the time comes when the child rebels at parental protection, seeing it as a limit to freedom. By that time, a child has missed many chances to increase in his or her own sense of competence while still enjoying the protection of parents. Such protection, very valuable to a small child, becomes a nuisance to an adolescent.

Almost from the moment of birth, an infant is capable of assuming some responsibility. The first sign to the adult is probably the baby's cry of hunger or discomfort. The baby learns quickly what happens as a result of an outcry: Someone comes, or no one comes. If someone comes to tend the infant, generally the crying stops. If no one comes, the crying continues and gets louder. From this foundation an infant begins to make sense of the world that surrounds her or him, and forms attitudes toward other people.

The infant becomes a toddler, then a kindergartener, then a schoolchild, and finally adolescence brings childhood to a close. All during this period the young person is preparing to become an adult. A child is not just a shorter person. There isn't one certain day when a boy can truthfully say, "Today I am a man" or a girl can say, "This marks the beginning of womanhood." There is an evolving process. It begins much earlier than we generally notice and continues at a much slower rate throughout life.

As parents, we are most helpful if we watch for signs of budding capabilities and assist our children in testing their capacities. While they are still young they need our protection and guidance. It is a disservice to children to "push them out of the nest," as birds are seen to do. Human children first need to be taught to go alone. It's much easier to refrain from doing things for them if we remember that we want to train our children to be as independent as possible. When the time comes for them to leave the nest, they are then as capable as childhood has allowed them to become. There will always be risks in life, but they will be prepared to take them.

For a child, occupation consists of both the tasks that he or she engages in on a daily basis, and the training for adult life that requires education and preparation. Thus education *is* the child's work and is to be treated as such. It should get the child ready to reach for her or his fullest potential. However, in a different sense than adult work, the child's work of learning is not limited to the eight-hour day or the five-day week, but can occur at any time. A young person is constantly absorbing information, impressions, and experiences that continually affect the ability to learn and perform.

Mindy, age five, came home from kindergarten in the early autumn and told her mother she had to bring samples of fallen leaves to school the next day. She was excited about her "homework" and felt important to have an assignment. However, she soon became more interested in her after-school snack and the afternoon TV programs, and did not gather the leaves.

The next morning Mrs. Armstrong, Mindy's mother, wanting to make sure that Mindy's assignment was done, ran out and picked up a dozen fallen leaves. She handed them to Mindy in a bag as the little girl left for school.

With this action, Mrs. Armstrong was telling Mindy without words that she didn't believe she was capable of carrying out an assignment and that she needed to lean on someone else. Already she taught her child that "School is too hard for you, but Mother will get you through." Mindy would perceive herself, as she probably had already begun to do, as always needing someone to do her work.

It would have been better for Mindy if her mother let her handle her own assignment. If Mindy did forget, she would learn the consequences of forgetting at an early age, and would have time to acquire new habits. A friendly way, conducive to Mindy's growth, would have been for Mrs. Armstrong to invite Mindy for a walk in the afternoon to look at the fallen leaves. Mindy would have the opportunity to pick leaves for school and gain the satisfaction of performing a task by herself on time.

Such mistaken assistance as Mrs. Armstrong gave is

given many times by conscientious parents, but it is better for the parents to wait to be asked for help; to let the child handle the assignments alone. With the performance of each task, a child grows in self-acceptance and self-confidence.

Love

Love habitually eludes definition; but we continue to try. It's good to feel and hard to describe. To an adult, the task of love arises from the "fact that we live in two sexes and that the continuance and furtherance of mankind depends on our love life."* The way a person chooses a mate as well as the way the relationship works is largely a result of early experiences and perceptions.

The example parents set is crucial to children. Young people observe how the parents relate to one another and at the same time form perceptions of themselves in relation to others. The way mother and father speak and act, not only to each other and to the child, but to other siblings, relatives, and the community at large, forms the matrix on which children mold the shape of their own unique concept of love.

Children learn about love as they grow. The strongest influences occur within the family during the very early years. In order to learn how to give love a child has to receive love. Particularly, a child discovers whether parents' love is or is not tied to approval of behavior. This is one of the earliest lessons: A parent may strongly disapprove of an act, and take action about it while demonstrating in other ways that parental love continues.

* Alfred Adler, *What Life Should Mean to You*, p. 7.

Bert, age three, tipped over a full wastebasket. It wasn't clear how it happened, but it seemed that he may have done it deliberately to get his mother's attention. When his mother, Mrs. Alton, noticed it, she said: "The stuff fell out! You'll have to pick it all up!" Her voice was insistent but not angry. Bert knew she meant business, and began to pick up the papers and waste as his mother watched him. When he finished, Mrs. Alton said, "That's a good job," and returned to what she had been doing. She did not keep on shouting at him; she did not scold him for interrupting her, nor did she accuse him of doing it out of spite. She did not call him a "bad boy." She called attention to the situation and required that Bert restore order. Since the emphasis was on what had to be done as a result of the act rather than on who committed it, her love for him was not in question. With a child of any age, it is always wise to limit one's comments to the situation and to require that it be corrected rather than to place blame, direct anger, or attribute "badness."

In this way a child learns what love is and what it means between people and among the members of a group such as a family. Even a baby perceives the attitudes that surround her or him and basks or frets in the atmosphere, depending on whether it is loving or cold.

Most parents have noticed the sharp perception of an infant or small child in tense moments. Why is it that when parents are hurried or harried a baby cries? Mothers notice that when they're trying to get ready to go out, the baby gets fussy. The baby senses, although it cannot yet understand language, that something different is in the air. In a similar sense, a baby will relax and coo when all is calm.

Demonstrations of affection accompany a loving attitude. All of us humans need the touch of other persons, and the younger a child is, the more a hug, a cuddle, a soft stroke is appreciated. Only the child who receives such touching can grow to be the adult who gives it. Therapists and counselors have histories of people who are unhappy adults, unable to show affection to their partners. Clients tell of childhood and family life in which people were cool and distant. They remark that they never saw nor received loving gestures and as adults they find it hard to learn how.

Friendship

As soon as a toddler leaves the family on a regular basis, friendship becomes important. We used to assume that the family was a child's whole life until kindergarten. With changes in individual roles and occupations has come a growth in nursery schools and other child-care arrangements. Today many young children spend their entire days outside the family, either in a formal day-care center or in the care of a baby-sitter at home or in another household.

Thus removed from family, the infant or toddler is exposed to a new set of circumstances, a different set of human beings, and different responses. A two-year-old, for instance, is only minimally independent and must look to the responsible person not only for food and diaper changes, but for care and nurture. This toddler soon discovers whether the behavior she or he produces within the family will get the desired response from the baby-sitter or attendant. If it does not, the toddler may behave differently. This accounts for the differences we often see in how a child behaves at home and away. It depends on who is nearby.

At this time, the child also begins to establish friendships with other children. Those youngsters with whom a child comes in contact regularly influence the habits, vocabulary, and activities of the individual. The friendships thus formed become another expression of the child's personality and assume greater importance as the child grows older. It is reasonable for a parent to know the other children, to be interested in them, and to help the child enjoy them. It is neither wise nor effective for a parent to attempt to choose the child's friends. The concept of friendship originates in these first early steps into the wider world outside the family. Even the child who spends most of the day at home with a parent does occasionally visit in other homes, meet children in the playground, and have encounters with different people. All of these relationships help to shape the child's personality. Children who see the world as a friendly place where they can feel secure will probably feel that it is good to trust others, to participate in and contribute to joint effort. Children who become afraid of the larger world, who feel threatened by it, are much more likely to feel that they are growing up in enemy territory. Such people must be ever watchful for attack and always prepared to defend. This illustrates only two exaggerated traits of personality: the person who is cheerful and the one who is fearful.

Although each stage of growth brings opportunities for greater independence, the young child is still mainly dependent on an adult. Putting on a jacket is a skill that some children can learn at age three, others not until age five. One of the things that determines how early the child learns to do it unaided is whether the adult does it for the child or whether he teaches the child how to do it alone. Even the youngster with little language learns early to say "M'self!" trying to put an arm in the sleeve; but if the adult does not foster the attempt, the eagerness dies fast. Sometimes the way the jacket fits, the way it fastens, and the way it is stored makes the difference between independence and dependence. Even the one who could put on last year's jacket easily may be stumped by a new one. Similarly, the kindergartener who could get the jacket from a low hook, put it on, and fasten it may become dependent when he or she is in a place where the jacket is out of reach. A loose jacket goes on more easily than a tight one. A separating zipper may be easy for a six-year-old but impossible for a four-year-old. Each child is at a different stage of ability, and it is important to take notice.

Although work, love, and friendship encompass most of the challenge of living, Adler mentioned other tasks, and some of his followers and interpreters have identified them. There is the fourth task, the existential, or that of getting along with one's self. The fifth task, the spiritual, is to consider man's relation to the universe. Both are tied to the establishment of values and priorities. The child is not likely to grapple with these concepts, but the foundation of understanding is laid in childhood. Therefore, parents have to consider and understand the values their children are absorbing. Sometimes the values we say we hold are not the same ones we demonstrate by the way we live. Children are more impressed by what we do than by what we say.

In helping a child prepare to become an independent, fulfilled adult, we want him or her to be equipped to cope with the tasks of work, love, and friendship; to be self-accepting; and to have an understanding of one's own relationship to the universe. Thus does a child gain the requisite traits for achievement.

4

Personal Goals: Self-Confidence, Self-Esteem, Self-Respect

As a child learns and grows, she or he continually makes decisions based on perceptions of self, the family, and the world. Most of the decisions are made automatically, without awareness. Thus is personality developed along with an individual perception of life.

In order for parents to help rather than hinder their children's development, it is wise to understand this process and learn how to act and what to say so that children get positive ideas about themselves and about life.

At birth, every infant feels almost insignificant because in fact a baby is almost totally dependent on others for its very existence. It is a living being wanting to survive and must learn how. In the human race, the young must look to adults for sustenance and protection over a very long period—longer than in any other species. Parents suddenly thrust into such a situation, where a living being is totally dependent on them, usually feel a tremendous sense of responsibility, but that feeling is not always pleasant.

One needs only to recall being awakened from a sound sleep by an infant's cry to remember groaning, and wishing that the baby could get its own food and comfort. On the other hand, the overwhelming sense of being needed also leads to a suffusion of wonder and well-being. The care of an infant brings out sets of opposing feelings. We like being essential to such a completely helpless person, giving us a tremendous feeling of importance, but we resent the interference in our own lives.

Most of us soon make the necessary adaptations so that the child receives the proper care and the adults learn to give it with less hostility. The rewards increase as the infant grows. Even at 2:00 A.M. the first smile looks good.

We are less aware of the importance of nurture for the psychological development of the child, and rarely understand the importance of the beginning relationship between the baby and the adults who care for her or him.

From the moment a child leaves the womb, it needs in addition to care, feeding, and nurture, training in becoming independent, for only the person who feels capable of self-mastery can become a fully functioning individual. The child needs to overcome her or his original feeling of insignificance and inferiority in order to attain self-confidence and with it the achievement of success.

As long as we live, all of us continue to strive for significance, and so it is difficult to imagine how much harder our little ones are striving, and what an effect our interaction with them has on their own perceptions. They need from us every possible encouragement that we can give them. What they don't need are the reminders of their own smallness. Of that they're well aware.

We can't know with any certainty just when an infant begins to mold its own personality, but we won't err if we assume it begins very, very early. All humans have inherent feelings of inferiority that lead to the striving we notice. Each one begins to perceive and draws simple conclusions from those perceptions. We contribute to their growth with every chance we allow for independent activity. The child develops within a continuity of relationships with others, constantly adding impressions and knowledge and organizing those bits of information into a unified personality.

The need for and the benefits of independence can be demonstrated in caring for an infant. Watching young Mrs. Sutton care for her baby, I saw her feeding her small son formula from a nursing bottle. She held the baby close in her arms, his head in the crook of her elbow as he sucked. In a while, he stopped sucking and turned his head away from her and the bottle, out toward the room. She commented that her first impulse was to follow his lips with the nipple, but she did not; she merely held it in the same position, waiting. In a few moments, having rested, the baby returned to the nipple and finished the bottle of formula. He had controlled the pace at which he ate, had made a decision about when to finish sucking, and had learned an early lesson in independence.

You can see a similar sign of independent action if you watch someone feeding a young baby with a spoon. I watched Mr. Fogarty feed little Norma as she sat in her high chair. When she turned her head away, Mr. Fogarty tried to follow her mouth with the spoon. She turned farther and he tried to catch her elusive lips. It looked like a real power struggle, each one trying to win. When he quit trying to force the food into her mouth, the war was over. A few moments later, when Norma began to repeat her behavior, he waited calmly for her to turn her head toward him, which she eventually did. It was much more pleasant for both of them.

A related situation often occurs when a small child plays quietly alone. If the child is in a playpen, the demonstration may be dramatic. Karen Russell, not quite one year old, was playing alone with her toy telephone, surrounded by other playthings. Her father came into the room, picked her up, spoke to her sweetly, cuddled her a moment, and then put her down within reach of her toys. He thought he was being a loving father, and was shocked when she began to scream. Her protest was a direct result of the interruption. She thought he was going to play with her a while and keep her company. Her outcry expressed her surprise and anger. He had not shown respect for her concentration, nor had he realized that he would be creating expectations within her.

Even very young children will concentrate for a long time in activities they themselves invent and undertake. The "short attention span" we hear of so often is more likely in activities imposed by someone else. Certainly it was appropriate for Mr. Russell to come into the room and speak to Karen, but if he wanted to take her out of the playpen and away from what she was doing, he should not have abruptly put her back.

Another common error was committed that evening when Mrs. Russell put Karen to bed at the usual hour but awakened her two hours later for the pleasure of showing her off to some friends who dropped in. Mrs. Russell was proud of her daughter; she didn't realize she was intruding on her until she heard the screams of protest when she put her back to bed.

These examples are shown with infants, because it is at

that time of life that it is easiest for parents to "manage" them. They have a great need for the care of parents, and they are small enough to be lifted, carried, thrown, and otherwise manipulated. With each incident, the child is forming impressions of himself or herself.

If a child is to develop feelings of self-respect, parents have to treat even a small baby with respect from the earliest days. Maybe it's an inconvenience to think of the child first, but it's minor compared to the joys that follow when respect flows both ways. It is the parents who are the most powerful teachers, especially in the very early years.

A child is not a possession to be displayed. The new baby, or even the older one, is not to be regarded as an acquisition in the same class as a hobby, such as a new lens for the camera or slides from the latest trip. Of course we parents have pleasure when others admire our young ones, but we must strike a balance between enjoying such admiration and seeking opportunities to get it. The danger in "showing off" is that the child will value such admiration so highly that she or he might go to any lengths to get it.

Seeking attention is one of the inappropriate goals that children develop as they view their relationships to their families and the world. Many children get the mistaken idea that they are only worthwhile if the people around them pay them constant attention. Such youngsters can make life miserable for everyone by constant demands, and make themselves unhappy as well. The child who is allowed as much independence as he or she can handle is much more likely to be cooperative than demanding.

Lavish praise can also create a problem. Praise is not always encouraging. If you make a big fuss over every drawing that comes home from kindergarten and post each one prominently in the kitchen what's left for first grade? Certainly each piece of work is valuable in a child's development, but overemphasis crowds out reality. The danger is that the youngster may get the idea that nothing he or she does is worth doing unless it elicits praise. The risk we take by too much emphasis on each achievement is that we lead children to believe that they must always do something special, or be noticed as someone special, in order to feel worthwhile.

Adults can help children to learn to value themselves as worthwhile human beings, capable of becoming more independent as they grow, and to have respect for themselves and others. We want them also to learn to live in harmony with others. All these tasks are harder for the person who has a low feeling of self-worth. The one who feels unworthy is likely to be hesitant, to lack the courage to get on with life's work.

Consider what happens when a preschooler gets hold of crayons. The marks the child makes are likely to be scrawls, but we're delighted if they appear on paper rather than on walls. Maybe the lines do resemble something we've seen, but they don't have to. The child is learning what happens when she or he holds this unusual little stick and presses it. By experiment, one learns to make different colors appear, to make bold marks. This is not the time for drawing precisely. Coloring books can be a hindrance. The lines printed are only to suggest figures to be filled in. When parents or teachers criticize because a child's crayon goes beyond the lines, the adults effectively discourage the child.

Jeffrey came from kindergarten one afternoon with four pages of work his teacher had assigned. Each page bore examples of shapes that the children were to match up and distinguish, in preparation for reading. They were to use their crayons to indicate which shapes matched. Jeffrey was proud that he had them all correct, and there was a big "100" at the top of the page, but he noticed some words that the teacher had written and asked his mother what they said. She read, "Poor coloring," and Jeffrey's elation vanished. The teacher ignored the fact that he was able to match up the forms well and called attention instead to the coloring that didn't stay inside the lines. Jeffrey's self-confidence received a nick.

The ability to draw comes to a child after repeated practice. The objective is for the child to feel free to continue, to enjoy the task at hand, and to improve as he or she does it. For instance, when a child is drawing pictures for fun and shows them to a parent, it isn't helpful to say, "What is it?" "I like it" is much more effective. If the child asks, "What color should I make the next one?" the answer can be, "Any color you like." Who said a purple hippopotamus won't be pretty? Ogden Nash wrote a famous poem about a purple cow, didn't he?

As children get older, if they've been squelched it will show in their approaches to new ideas or new challenges. A school-age child has already formed consistent patterns of behavior and response. It is not too late, however, for a parent to notice and to act in a different, more encouraging way.

We must remember that the perceptions children form in the early years are not necessarily accurate, and that their beliefs about themselves and their connection to others can yet change. They continue to need opportunities for independent action, to experience the respect of others so that they may have self-respect, and to learn the value of cooperation.

Among the basic errors in beliefs that people make about themselves, starting in childhood, are these:

"I am only worthwhile if I am perfect."

"The world is against me."

"Life is a continual battle."

"Unless I am superior to other people, I remain inferior."

"I can only survive if I have a constant protector."

"Unless others always pay attention to me, I am not worthy."

"I am only significant if I have my own way."

"I must win."

"I have value only when others serve me."

"I am alone in the world, and inept."

This is a very small sample of some of the mistaken ideas people invent at an early age and carry along through life. None of them needs to be true, but each of them acts as an inhibitor to the full pursuit of life and achievement. They are set out here to illustrate the varieties of mistakes children make. Any of them creates obstacles to emotional and mental growth and all of them are subject to change and correction. It isn't necessary to analyze your child in order to learn how to help him or her. It is only necessary to understand the way such mistaken ideas cramp the development of self-confidence. Then you can take the actions and say the words that will help a child overcome such obstacles.

To be successful, a person needs the confidence that comes from feeling good enough, feeling like a valued member of the family and community, and a willing participant in the challenges life brings. Helping your child along these lines may also help you to discover that you too can blossom in an encouraging atmosphere. Parenting isn't a one-way activity directed at children; it can bestow unexpected rewards upon the parents as well.

5

Interpersonal Relationships

How can parents contribute to the vitality of the interpersonal relationships a child forms? That's the question this chapter will consider. First we must recognize how many different ways there are that each human being interacts with others. Everyone forms personality traits in interaction with a social group, that is, other people, learning from their responses. No human being is one-dimensional, and every connection with another person is shaped by both parties.

Within the Family

We cannot begin to list all the different groups a person takes part in, but we realize the special importance of the first group; that is, the family into which a child is born. For a first-born, this usually consists of just two adults, as in the line from an old song, " . . . and baby makes three."* Other family members may arrive, changing the

* From "My Blue Heaven," lyrics by George Whiting, music by Walter Donaldson, copyright © 1927 Leo Feist.

numbers, the structure, and the patterns of interaction. If a child joins a family that already consists of one or more siblings, this new addition affects them and the interaction changes.

The new member only knows the family as he or she finds it, and quickly learns the roles of the others. Then the child adopts ways to behave with those people in order to fit in and function. Every parent, of course, has the most control of his or her own behavior and less influence on how the others act toward the newborn, the growing child, and each other.

The Greene family is a good illustration. Mr. and Mrs. Greene have a son Harlan, age four, and a new baby daughter named Heather. If we try to count the bonds between and among them, we can count at least a dozen connections, each slightly different from all the others. We see the two-way relationship between the adults. Then there are those that develop between Harlan and Heather; Harlan with his father and with his mother; Heather similarly with each parent separately; and the variations that depend on how many family members are present at any one time. Each relationship is shaped by events and by the differing perceptions and responses of each individual. Different behavior at different times produces different results, and all the relationships are affected in many ways.

Most parents wonder how big a part they play in helping their children get along together. In the family they want to provide for loving and permanent attachments between their children. Probably all fathers and mothers want their children to be lifelong comrades to each other, and they make many mistakes trying to ensure that result. It becomes apparent very early that siblings form their own opinions of one another, and they may not agree with those their elders hold. Adults have to accept their own limitations, allowing brothers and sisters to find their own ways to live as siblings and to work out their disagreements among themselves. They test, they risk, and they discover how to get along together—often in ways that do result in pleasure for their parents. If parents do not get involved in the differences and conflicts between and among their children, there is less need for the children to wrangle. They become freer to solve their problems as they grow. In this as in other aspects of family life, parents set an example; for children look to them as role models and copy some of their attitudes, adding their own modifications and revisions.

Rather than attempting to impose caring on their children, parents can help the whole family learn to live in harmony with the technique of the regular family meeting, or the "Family Council." Many other names are used by different families, such as "Round Table," "Regular Session," "Directors' Meeting," or just "Meeting." The term *Family Council* comes from the translation of *Familienrat*, the German word used by Alfred Adler to describe the process.

Briefly, a Family Council is a regular meeting of all the members of a family that live together, whether or not they are biologically related. It meets on a regular schedule that is agreed upon in advance by everybody, and its purpose is for the members to communicate with one another in an effort to solve the inevitable problems that arise in daily living.

Its operating procedure provides that each person has an opportunity to speak without interruption and without receiving criticism; and that each person has a turn to be the one who keeps order, variously called "monitor," "chairperson," or "leader." Records, like minutes, are kept at the discretion and decision of the family members.

During the meeting time of the Family Council, parents and other adults forfeit their authority. Parents do not act as judges in handing down decisions; rather, everyone decides together how the family will solve a problem. Meetings are held regularly, even when there is no pressing problem, in order to assure the continuity of the gathering together.

One of the very productive aspects of Family Council is that the family can plan for fun together, from the simplest game after a meeting to elaborate plans for a family vacation. Another aspect of family life that operates in the Family Council is the assumption of responsibility for necessary chores. Instead of parents assigning jobs to children, all family members participate in the preparation of a list of household tasks and the allotment of them to individuals or teams.

When the jobs cease to be "helping mother with her duties" and become instead the work that must be done so that the family can eat, wear clean clothes, and keep the household going, even very young children become more interested in assuming their personal share of the burden.

As conflicts arise in the family, the Family Council is an excellent atmosphere in which to attempt to solve them, although it is generally unwise to call family meetings only for such a purpose. The family needs the regular sessions to train themselves to talk to one another freely and without rancor. Then when a problem erupts, there is a format within which to deal with it.

Conflicts between people rarely are about what they say they are anyway. What seems to be the issue in the height of the argument is rarely the real issue. Rather the real issue underlies the conflict between the people who are fighting. The real issue in each person's mind is likely to be something like one of these:

"Who's winning this one?"
"Am I always the loser, the underdog?"
"Is it going to be my way or his?"
"Can she make me do it?"
"I can't admit I may be wrong."
"I can't let them know I'm afraid."

Anger and fear, resentment and revenge are uppermost in each person's mind, and mask the actual issues. These emotions provide fuel for the engines that push the fight machinery. But there are steps toward solution of a conflict.

The basic step is to create an attitude of mutual respect. It isn't there when the argument starts, but it can be produced, especially if the family has been practicing such respect for one another in meetings and in family life in general when there is no conflict.

Then the real issue must be narrowed down to the immediate cause of disagreement. Often in a dispute each party will reach back in memory for past injustices and pile them on in hopes of making the present argument stronger. However, the conflict can only be solved on the basis of the immediate differences. Even during the fight, there is cooperation—each party contributes to keeping the fight going. So it is a small step to the kind of cooperation that leads to agreement: deciding what the real issue is.

When the real issue is illuminated, the task of finding areas of agreement begins. There are always some aspects of the differences that a person is willing to concede. They are found when the search is conducted in an atmosphere of trust and respect. Attempts by anyone to put down anyone else will only make it harder to solve the problem. No one wants to lose face, and no one wants to feel put down.

If agreement still cannot be reached, the best approach is to postpone the subject until the next family meeting. By that time, anger will be defused and the persons involved will be much less insistent on their particular points. Any conflict can be put aside for a later date. In a real emergency, there would be no conflict. People don't say "Why?" if someone shouts, "Get out! The house is on fire!"

Assuming that agreement is reached and the conflict is resolved, a decision has to be made as to how the agreement will be carried out. To complete the solution, the responsibilities for further action are to be shared by all.

In the book *Family Council*, by Rudolf Dreikurs, Shirley Gould, and Raymond J. Corsini, the procedure for family meetings, the reasons for having them, and the methods for conducting them, as well as ways of conflict-solving, are set out in much greater detail. Read it to prepare for beginning the system in your own home.

Outside the Family

Beyond the limits of the family, there are many other interpersonal relationships for each child. Every encounter, every experience contributes to the formation of a child's personality and outlook on life. The perceptions and attitudes a child forms within the family are the ones she or he uses in relationships with the people and the world outside the home. What the parents do and say and the perceptions they express about a child are of great early influence in those attitudes.

One of the greatest mistakes an adult can make is to put offspring into categories, to label them according to their attributes or abilities. It may seem inevitable that a mother or father will think, "She certainly is bright," or "He's so good with his hands." You don't have to walk a tightrope in guarding your words, but it is good to be aware of the possible outcomes.

For instance, Dr. Henderson was telling me about his children, whom I had not yet met. He said, "Eric, my oldest son, will surely be a scientist. He's so smart and gets such good grades, I just know he'll be a success in an academic profession and make a name for himself. But I'm not so sure about Lewis. He just doesn't seem to have any interest in studying, or in getting good grades, no matter how I try to help him. Because he's good with his hands, I think, I'll buy an old junk car and teach him to fix it. Then he can always be an auto mechanic, and that pays pretty well."

When he spoke of his only daughter, Dr. Henderson's voice became soft. "Eunice is so pretty, we don't have to worry about her. Of course, I'll see that she gets an education so she'll have something to fall back on, but she'll marry young and be a real asset to some young man's career."

It is obvious that Dr. Henderson was expressing prejudice against women, and he didn't deny that; but what he didn't realize was how his views affected the children and their regard for one another, besides their own opportunities for development and their individual self-esteem.

When I met them, I found Eric to be both arrogant and timid. He was afraid he might not live up to the very high expectations expressed for him, and at the same time he realized that his was the loftiest place in the family. He looked down on Lewis, who felt discouraged and resented Eric's eminence. He said, "Why should I try to make good grades? I couldn't ever catch up to Eric anyway." Eunice, not only pretty but the "baby" of the family, expected service from her brothers, and concentrated her efforts on getting it and on enhancing her good looks. She didn't seem to think she had to do anything to prepare for adult life.

What about Mrs. Henderson? She deferred to her husband since she had been trained to be the subordinate partner. Her beauty is the adult version of Eunice's prettiness, and she's very careful to preserve it, recognizing it as her main asset.

In the interpersonal relationships that Eric, Lewis, and Eunice form, both among themselves and outside the family, their views are shaped by what they hear and experience at home. Such attitudes do not contribute to the achievement of success, since each child feels limited by the prescriptions their father wrote for them.

Certainly it's no crime to notice your children's strengths and to take pride in them. The error is in talking about them as if they're permanent and unchangeable. That makes it much harder for the children to explore other avenues of development, to seek to learn other skills, to try new tasks. If a child knows that his value depends on high grades in academic subjects, he'll be much less likely to try out for basketball. Or if she hears her parents say they don't expect her to learn math, she's not likely to enroll for algebra if she doesn't have to.

We all wonder what they'll be like when they grow up, and we fantasize the Nobel Prize winner, the statesman, the great beauty, the successful banker. We can assume that the children dream too, but we must be sure always to maintain a light, even a humorous, touch if we talk about those fantasies. "Will you take me for a ride in your speedboat?" is a question I used to ask my twelve-year-old son when he talked about how rich he planned to be when he grew up, and what toys he'd buy.

Looking outside the family, we often disapprove of the friendships our children make. We worry about how their peers will influence and affect their lives. Often we feel overpowered by such influences. We worry even more if they don't seem to make many friends. As in the relationships between siblings, parents have to keep hands off as much as possible.

Already, the choices we made have shaped our children's opportunities. We chose where to live, where the children attend school, and our other associations such as churches, clubs, and community activities. In doing so, we have either limited or expanded our children's chances to become acquainted with others whose lives may be different from their own.

In general, the influences of home will be stronger than those outside. When on occasion it appears that an acquaintance may actually be leading one of our children toward unacceptable behavior, we must be cautious in our reaction. Depending on how old and how astute a child is, our opposition will push the child closer to the disapproved one. Express your disapproval, refuse to do anything you feel is wrong, but do not issue edicts or decrees that you can't enforce.

For instance, you don't have to drive the car to take your youngster to meet a friend or a group of which you disapprove. You don't have to provide hospitality to someone you don't want in your house. But you can't very well say, "I forbid you ever to speak to her again," for, let's face it: You have no way of following through.

A strong influence on every person is the desire to be a valuable part of a group. Many children seek this outside the home if they don't find it in the family circle. A child first learns that at home there are certain standards, habits, and values that may differ from those outside. The youngster needs to have the certainty that the family values her or him as a person, that this is one group with whom he or she belongs. This is not to say that person is owned by others; that's not what I mean by "belong." Each of us needs to know that we fit. We need to know we are accepted, with all our faults, by our own families. If we don't find such acceptance at home, we'll look for it elsewhere.

Some of the attitudes that destroy such knowledge for a young child are comparisons between brothers and sisters, unrealistic expectations of achievement, and emphasis on differences. The attitudes that contribute to a feeling of acceptance are those that encourage each child to be an individual, to reach for growth, and to express her or his ideas and wishes.

To honor one's own family is not to put other families down. Nothing is gained by a motto that says "We're better." On the contrary, as with individuals, such assertions of superiority are likely to mask feelings of inferiority.

A healthy family atmosphere, conducive to the well-being of all members, accepts each member as a valuable person and recognizes the unique qualities of one family without raising or lowering it in comparison to others. The family members then can have a feeling of belonging to one another and to the group.

As in other aspects of personality, if a child has developed self-confidence and there is mutual respect among family members, adults and children, you can trust that the interest in an unsuitable person will be of short duration and minimal harm. The child will learn from the experience. Often such friendships are deliberately entered into by a child to gain revenge on a parent or both parents. If decrees are issued, it's fun for a child to defy them.

The world presents many different kinds of people, and we all have to live together for the time being on this limited planet. Our children will probably outlive us, and it is for their good that they learn early how to meet and relate to people outside the family. In the family atmosphere, through open discussion they can decide which people to choose for close friends, how to handle those friendships, and also how to cope with the inevitable disappointments of connections broken or outgrown.

Children adapt to new situations. For instance, when it becomes necessary to move the household, listen to your children's ideas as well as their protests. When they understand that the move is inevitable, they can tell you how to help them make it. They may even tell you how you can make life pleasant in the new place.

For example, the Mesigals had an unexpected experience in their move from one end of the town to the other. The parents assumed that the children would want to stay in their old familiar school until the end of the school year. Mrs. Mesigal offered to make the round trip twice daily so that Alex, ten, in fifth grade, and Janice, twelve, in seventh, could be with their friends until summer. Alex refused her offer, saying, "If the new school is like ours, when a new kid comes in during the year the teacher makes a special point to see that he's introduced to everyone, and appoints someone to help him find out whatever he needs to know. If a new kid comes in at the beginning of the school year in the fall, he's just one in the crowd getting used to a new room and new teacher. I want to go to the new school as soon as we move, so I can get that special introduction to new friends."

Janice listened carefully, even though she was the one who usually instigated new ideas. She had seen the big junior high she would attend, with three times as many pupils as her "old" school, and knew they had a system of changing classes for every subject. She decided to transfer too, as soon as the family moved.

This is only one example of the helpful ideas that children will articulate if they know that adults will listen and take them seriously. Despite their reluctance to move and leave their friends, Alex and Janice knew they had no choice. Thus they sought the best way to get acquainted with the new surroundings and to make new friends. Similarly, children will learn to handle interpersonal relationships outside the family if they have the freedom to do so.

6
Courage: Its Many Meanings

We'd need a whole book on courage to explore its many meanings and to understand the impact of a lack of courage on a human being. The word itself comes from the French word for heart, *coeur*. Like the heart, courage is essential to the human. Without it, life is bleak. Some of us have it to a greater degree than others, some in different types of courage, but we need courage in many ways if we are to function at more than the level of mere existence.

Defining Courage

One of the definitions of courage is "mental or moral strength to venture, persevere, and withstand danger, fear, or difficulty." We usually think of courage as the art of being brave in a crisis, and we rarely associate it with the conduct of our everyday lives. But when we make courage an integral part of everything we do and think, we enrich ourselves and expand our own possibilities.

In writing about creativity, Rollo May, the eminent psychiatrist and theoretician, in *Courage to Create* identifies four different kinds of courage, describing them all as essential to being human. Enumerating them, he speaks first of physical courage, "the simplest and most obvious kind." When we think of bravery, that is physical courage. Next, he lists moral courage, what we might call "the courage of our convictions." When a person takes an unpopular view and risks criticism for it, we often admire him or her for having such courage. Some of us have it at times, when we feel very strongly about a subject. May then writes of the concept of social courage. He calls it the "courage to relate to other human beings." This is close to what we call "social interest," involvement with other people and the willingness to contribute to the welfare of the group. Adler called it *Gemeinschaftsgefühl,* usually translated as "social interest," but recently it has been called "humanistic identification," indicating that we connect ourselves with other persons and identify ourselves with them in a humanistic fashion. Such a view asserts the dignity and worth of human beings.

The fourth kind of courage that May notes is the one he calls "creative courage." He says it is the most important, and describes the work of artists, musicians, and poets who create anew; that is, they create works of art which have never existed before. This kind of courage is especially necessary in times of change, he says, and only those who have it can successfully produce new ideas, new forms, and new understanding for themselves and for others.

The Courage to Be Imperfect

It is not necessary here to decide which of the various kinds of courage is most important, but we will consider the courage to be imperfect, which is an aspect of creative courage and essential to all creativity. Not many of us will become artists, musicians, or poets, but all of us need the courage to be imperfect in our daily lives. We are creating constantly, as each day brings forth new challenges. Every hour we live is a new creation, and although we may assume we're merely repeating habits of the past, we are in effect re-creating at every moment.

This is important to understand, because children more than adults are continually doing, thinking, or learning something for the very first time, each in his or her own unique way. We acknowledge this as adults when we are awed as if we were children, or when we attempt to learn something new and experience the kind of fear and bewilderment we first knew as young children.

If we want our children to become achievers, it is essential that we help them develop the courage to be less than perfect, so that they can meet such "firsts" and so that they will think, learn, and move toward success.

Perfection is such an elusive goal. Even if it can be attained, enjoyment of it requires someone else to notice, or at least to acknowledge it. Otherwise, the tremendous effort seems unnecessary. On the other hand, the performance of a task, no matter how imperfectly, can bring satisfaction by itself. Think about Dean, age seven, happily building a bridge with his Erector set. He doesn't know anything about the principles of construction, but by trial and error he gets it to hold together and to look like a bridge. He's done it all alone, and feels great that he did. He never tried a bridge before, and this one looks good to him.

Dean's father comes down to the family room, where Dean is admiring his bridge. Mr. Langley is a trained engineer and very handy around the house. He takes one look at the bridge and tells Dean it isn't straight. Then he takes it all apart and rebuilds it accurately, "to show Dean how to do it the right way." All the enjoyment Dean had in building the bridge is spoiled when his father takes it down. Later, Mrs. Langley wonders why Dean isn't interested in the Erector set anymore. When she asks Dean, he doesn't tell her because he doesn't want to be disloyal to his father, and he knows his father's intentions were good.

If Mr. Langley's standard allowed for imperfection, he might have been able to help Dean build the next structure, showing him how to make the next bridge stand straighter. By taking Dean's bridge down and doing it over, he not only lost an opportunity to encourage his son, but also put a lid on Dean's wish to learn more about building.

What other consequences are there when a person lacks the courage to be imperfect? Courage is not the absence of fear; it is the determination to act in spite of fear, against one's fear.

A common example is the person who is afraid of flying but goes on an airplane anyway. Like other worthy human attributes, courage requires choice. We have to consider the alternatives and choose. Bill and Harold were going to the same meeting in a distant city. Both were afraid to fly. Bill decided to go by air anyway and was in the other city in four hours. Harold decided he'd take the train and arrived there two days later. Each man had lacked courage, but their decisions were different. As in all aspects of living, there was choice and risk.

A different example is more pertinent to achievement. The person who is afraid to be wrong will typically deliberate carefully and hesitate before speaking. One university professor I know sometimes lectures on radio programs. He's very well versed in his subject, but he speaks so slowly and with so much hesitation that it's hard to follow his message. One day I asked him to tell me why he speaks that way, since his ordinary conversation is not so slow. He replied, "On the radio, I have to make sure I get everything exactly right." If he had the courage to be imperfect, he could get his ideas across much more effectively. In his care to be perfect, he loses his listeners. If your child hesitates to speak up the classroom, or cannot give a correct answer even when he or she knows it, consider the possibility of the same fear the professor has.

We all seek perfection because basically we all strive to get ahead. There's nothing wrong with that. What damages us is setting perfection as a standard, for no one can live up to it. Trying to reach such a high standard produces tension, and uses up effort that might be put to other uses. That does not mean we ought to perform all our tasks in a slipshod manner. We want to try to do well but not reproach ourselves when we don't. If we constantly measure ourselves by the standard of perfection, we will always come up short, disappointed, finding fault. In fact, sometimes we keep moving the standard higher, with the mistaken notion that we won't strive if the target is too easy to reach.

With our children, we often set such high standards for them that we can always find something to criticize, some way to remind them they aren't perfect. We therefore demean them, "put them in their place" as if they didn't know they were smaller and younger and less capable than we are.

Whether or not we believe in a deity, we can assume that perfection is achieved only by superior powers. A supernatural force—God—can create perfection, but human beings cannot. We may see perfection in the petals of a flower, for instance, but how many petals are actually perfectly shaped and completely without blemish? When we look at a bunch of blossoms, if we like them we're pleased. We're not likely to examine every petal closely to see if each blossom is perfect. It's the total effect that counts.

With our children, however, we're not very often satisfied with them *as they are*. We mistakenly examine everything they do and comment on most of it. We inspect their appearance, their conduct, and try to inspect what goes on in their minds. In our attempts to improve them, we often stifle their creativity, that unique quality that is in each of us.

It's not only a waste to try for perfection, but seeking it acts as a hindrance. The piano teachers of my youth insisted that each piece had to be played perfectly, by memory, before any of us could advance to another piece of music. They must have made some allowances, or I would have quit sooner than I did, but the effect of such great expectations was to give it up. I was unable to reach perfection, became discouraged, and didn't touch the piano again for thirty years. Recently, having developed the courage to be imperfect, I became able to learn to play the piano again. I won't perform in public, but I have great enjoyment from mastering the music I can play. Not perfectly, but passably.

Vladimir Horowitz, who comes as close to perfect piano playing as anyone, has been quoted as saying that each time he performs it is a new interpretation. He does not listen to his recordings in order not to be influenced by them. Maybe he even fluffs a note sometimes. Other concert pianists do. Isn't it odd that we persist in demanding perfection from ourselves and our children?

The person who lacks the courage to be imperfect is hampered in many ordinary acts. Such a person is afraid to try something new for fear of not doing it well. When we see this in adults, we accept it as part of a personality; but often when we see it in our children, we wring our hands and try to persuade. As in earlier examples, courage is not the absence of fear, but the determination to act in spite of fear. The fear of poor performance is rooted in the fear of disapproval. If as parents we do not disapprove, we help our children overcome such fears.

Children who are labeled by their parents with special attributes or weaknesses are likely to be bound by the fears of making new attempts. For example, the children of Dr. Henderson (mentioned in chapter 5) generally stay within the boundaries of the categories their father has imposed on them. Eric has said that he'd like to learn to make things with his hands, maybe take a class in woodworking at school. But then, he said, what if he couldn't do the woodworking as well as he does his science projects, or as well as his father does? Eric knew his father would disapprove and Eric himself would be disappointed.

Why should Eric expect to do everything well? Who knows what he might learn from woodworking, even poorly done? If he could acquire the kind of courage that would let him make an error, he'd feel free to try anything that interests him. He might not make a perfect chair in woodworking class any more than Dean made a perfect bridge with his Erector set, but he'd have the satisfaction of doing it. Then he could sort out for himself how he wants to spend his time and effort.

Eric's brother Lewis turned away from schoolwork after he realized how his father's labels applied to him. Now, knowing (or believing) that he can't understand the printed word as quickly as his brother can, he concentrates on other interests—areas in which he knows he can do well. He fixes things, and he makes new ones. Most of the time he's content, but since he doesn't have the courage to be imperfect, he sometimes gets angry. If Lewis finds he can't repair something for lack of the proper part, he feels frustrated and abandons the project. The frustration arises out of his own conviction that he ought to be able to do anything he tackles, and to do it perfectly. Lewis could have the impetus and the energy to persevere, to figure out a different way to reach his objective, if he wasn't expecting so much of himself.

Life is full of stumbling blocks. The difference between the person who achieves and the one who gives up shows at such points. The achiever will go on with the job, despite a temporary setback. If the obstacle is too high, the achiever will go around instead of over it. The discouraged person surrenders.

A common complaint of parents is children who beg for lessons in music, art, or sports, and then give up after their parents have invested a lot of money in the instrument, the equipment, and the lessons. A mother or father often makes personal sacrifices to buy a clarinet or a guitar and to pay for lessons, only to have the youngster lose interest in a short time. One of the causes of such loss of interest is exaggerated expectations. Linnea, age six, wanted to play the piano. There was a piano at home, and when Linnea learned to read she thought that piano playing would be a simple matter of learning to read music. She thought her first lesson would teach her to play, and when it was over, she was crushed. Her own expectations led to her disillusionment. She found there was a lot to learn both in her head and in her fingers before she could play the way her teacher did. Her enthusiasm diminished, and she had to revise her own expectations or abandon the attempt to learn.

Fortunately, Linnea's piano teacher understood the child's plight and adjusted her curriculum so that Linnea discovered she could learn simple melodies as she continued to work toward greater proficiency. With this kind of adult direction, Linnea would achieve her goal.

The achiever knows that there will be setbacks, that mistakes are inevitable but not impenetrable. The achiever knows that to complete a task is better than to stop because the work isn't perfect. We could have the motto emblazoned in our homes and work places to remind us that "finished is better than perfect."

What is the parent's role? To accept your child, your children, *as they are*, complete with imperfections, blemishes, and limitations. This does not mean that you allow yourself to become discouraged by their limitations. You realize that growth comes in directions you cannot possibly foresee. In order to reach such growth, children need to have the knowledge that you are willing to watch them try and that you will not berate them if they fall short of your expectations. It is better to allow children to do for themselves anything they can rather than for adults to do it for them. If a toddler puts her shirt on backward, for instance, it is more helpful for the adult to commend her on the attempt rather than to take it off and put it on right. You know how, but the child has to learn.

One of the most damaging statements people make to one another, adult to adult as well as adult to child, is to say, "I told you so." Many times it's true, but that doesn't take away the sting. No one wants to be reminded that someone else knew better all the time. Most of us prefer to find out for ourselves, and children especially learn best when they are allowed the freedom to discover. To say "I told you so" is to assert one's superiority. The next time you want to say it, stop and think. What is your purpose?

Do you think the child doesn't remember your earlier words? He or she probably does, and all you want to do is emphasize your superiority.

Of course we make mistakes; if we don't, we've taken no action. Without action, we don't move. Without movement, we don't learn, and then we're stagnant. Children, however, are never stagnant. They're learning all the time, making decisions about themselves, the world, and about us. They are continually moving into new stages of growth, both biological and emotional, and if we want them to achieve, we have to help them acquire the necessary courage.

They will develop courage if we let them.

7
Energy for Perseverance

Earlier, in stating the requirements for achievement, I said that one of the necessary components is the energy to persevere. In discussing the courage to be imperfect, I stressed the importance of task completion and some of the causes and effects of quitting. Throughout this book, I refer mainly to emotional attitudes, and the relationships between parents and children that shape them.

However, children need physical energy too, and parents have limited ability to help them get it. You can't buy a bottle of stamina and inject it with a hypodermic needle. Neither can you instill staying power by what you tell a child. There are some things you can do. You can be alert to the signs that a child's energy is decreasing. You can supply the necessities for restoring energy and the atmosphere conducive to its maintenance. The achiever needs to be able to do whatever is called for in life situations, and the supply of physical energy is essential.

The achiever needs good nutrition, healthy habits, and appropriate medical care. In a changing culture, parents need to consider how the conditions of the home and family life contribute to or detract from those qualities. Opportunites for us to assist our children and to meet their requirements are abundant. But there are just as many chances for our children to resist our efforts and hurt their physical beings. Each one has innate physical energy, but the very nature of childhood is constant growth, which can deplete it. Illness saps energy, as we all know, but we're less aware of the harm done by inadequate or improper nutrition and inadequate or inappropriate activity.

Parental responsibility has shifted. A century ago, survival was parents' main challenge. It took maximum effort to feed, clothe, and shelter a family. Now those needs are more easily met and we have to look out for the physical needs of our children in more subtle ways.

When life required hard physical labor, there was neither time nor opportunity for parents to consider the level of their children's physical energy. If we can imagine what life was like a hundred years ago, without electricity and the motors it runs, it's not hard to realize that every member of the family had to contribute effort and energy just to keep the group alive, fed, housed, and reasonably clean.

Without refrigerators, getting food on the table was a daily, difficult job. In the city, someone had to go to market every day, and in the country food had to be grown and stored. Before electric and gas stoves, wood had to be cut and carried to make fires for cooking and heating. Before washing machines, someone had to scrub the clothes on a washboard. Children were naturally expected to take on suitable chores as soon as they could.

Today, when we watch museum demonstrations of the crafts of spinning, weaving, candle dipping, and soap making, it is hobby work, like a game. But it wasn't fun when it was necessary to life. Everything the family needed required labor. Even the residue of the fires, the ashes, had to be carried away. In city apartments, that meant another trip down the stairs and up again. Today one of the most-mentioned jobs in the household is the continually filled garbage container. Its disposal is a constant irritant. Mother expects father to take care of it, he assigns the job to one of the children, and everybody grumbles.

Our way of living provides very little necessary physical activity and there is no reason why it should. Nobody wants to go back to a time of drudgery. But the technological advances that have freed us from hard work have also tempted us to sit around and "do nothing." In earlier times, child play was likely to be spontaneous and unorganized. There were few toys and fewer amusements. Children of this age, mesmerized by televised entertainment, sit or lie around. This does not contribute to a vigorous physical condition, since the growing body of a youngster requires active use of the developing muscles.

A parent can enhance a child's physical energy by providing plenty of opportunity for physical activity. Schools generally offer physical education, but many parents protect their children unnecessarily from its rigors. All active play doesn't have to be organized. Some of the best fun is invented by children just jumping and running. Not many of us have a hayloft to jump from, but we can provide an old mattress in the basement. Within the limitations of space and sound, children need freedom to move around.

Similarly, the child who eats casually may lack essential nutrients for health. The one who lacks restful sleep may fall asleep in the classroom. The child who does not receive recommended immunizations may succumb to a disease that could have been avoided.

A parent's obligation is basic for mealtime, bedtime, and medical care.

Eating together as a family is not always easy, but mealtime can contribute to the well-being of everyone in many ways besides the taking in of food. A pleasant atmosphere can not only assure enjoyment of the food but help to create a spirit of companionship. Everyone's self-confidence can expand in such a climate. Mealtime is not the time to create conflict by constant reminders, but neither is it necessary to allow chaos.

Mrs. Newlander asked me, "How can I teach Mark and Claire table manners if not at mealtime?" The best way is to set a good example. I told her, "Don't expect them to stay at the table until the meal is over if your husband is taking telephone calls, or if you get up and down several times." She responded, "But I have to get up to serve them!" Not necessarily. I told her to make sure everything is on the table before she sits down. Then, if anyone asks for something that isn't there, let that person get it.

Her husband's telephone calls are an annoyance to be discussed at the Family Council meetings. One possible arrangement would be an agreement that no one would allow an interruption during mealtime. Devices are available to shut off a telephone, or a call can be answered quickly with a statement that it will be returned after mealtime.

The time to discuss this type of conflict is at the meeting, not at the table. Attempting solutions during the disturbance is what makes conflicts harder to solve.

Mrs. Newlander was more concerned about her children's eating habits, and said, "It takes Claire so long to finish. She's four, and she can handle her fork well, but it seems she deliberately dawdles, and I have to keep on reminding and threatening her. Then I get angry, and it spoils the meal for all of us." I told her that instead of repeating the complaints, she can calmly say, "I guess you're not very hungry this time," and remove Claire's plate at the time everyone else finishes. Claire will learn soon that she's expected to eat in a reasonable time. Of course, she can't have anything to eat afterward if she is to learn.

"But then," Mrs. Newlander said, "she'll be in the kitchen all evening, snacking." Not if there aren't any snacks available. The best way to remove the temptation of junk food is to keep it out of the house. It isn't necessary to buy anything a child asks for. Better to risk a scene in the supermarket than to give in to the pleas for sweets featured in television commercials.

It may even be necessary to supervise Claire's after-meal hours more closely for a while in order to prevent her from getting food. That would still be less irritating and more productive than hollering at her all the time.

Bedtime is a difficult time in many families, but it can be simplified. There should be an orderly routine for the end of the day, but the children need to participate in planning it. This, too, is a topic for a Family Council meeting. Generally, parents will want children to go to sleep earlier than the children think is necessary. When reasonable agreement has been reached, parents can require that children stay in their beds, but cannot force sleep on them. Harmony will be maintained in the home when the children discover that the parents mean to protect their own privacy. It may be necessary at first to take a child by the hand back to bed, kindly but firmly. Each child should be taught at an early age to do his or her own undressing, washing, and preparing clothes for the morning. When a mother does it, or hovers over the child, she makes it more difficult for the child to learn self-reliance, and thus does a disservice.

In order for bedtime to be regular and orderly, there ought not to be very many occasions when children are kept up or away from home for the parents' convenience. Such an event should be a special one, and understood as such. Particularly on school nights, a regular bedtime procedure needs to be followed.

Maintenance of physical health requires periodic visits to a pediatrician or health care center to ensure that proper preventive measures are taken and that symptoms of illness are treated correctly. The child will accept these steps as a normal part of living if the parent does. The danger is for a parent to make such a fuss out of routine preventive care or of illness that the child uses it to get undue attention and concern. In the Bernstein family, when any of the children get sick, there is a dramatic upsurge in the attention Mrs. Bernstein gives. Orrin, the youngest, is ten, and has perfected a system that their pediatrician calls "secondary gain." We Adlerians recognize it as the use of his condition for the purpose of getting what he wants. He keeps his mother constantly busy with him and gets attention and service he doesn't think he can get any other way. He feels important as he sees his mother running back and forth to wait on him. The trouble is that he thus prolongs his inactivity, falls further behind in his schoolwork, and loses contact with his friends. He believes, incorrectly, that he is only significant and important when he can command such service.

His brother Seth, age twelve, seems to get just as many colds and other illnesses, but he doesn't capitalize on them, and so he spends very little time incapacitated. Mrs.

Bernstein feels sorry for Orrin but not for Seth, who accepts "being sick" but doesn't prolong it. So far, Seth is the achiever.

By feeling sorry for Orrin, his mother actually belittles him. By her actions, she communicates the message that he is incapable of fending for himself and needs the service and protection of his mother. This makes it additionally difficult for Orrin to have self-confidence.

Another common complaint is the one Mr. Platt made when he said to me, "My daughter Abby is just plain lazy." My first suggestion was that nine-year-old Abby have a complete and thorough physical examination. She might have a low-grade infection or some insufficiency that could cause her to seem lazy when actually her physical health was poor. When the medical diagnosis was okay, I talked to Abby at length to discover how she felt about herself and life. As with most children called "lazy," Abby's predominant idea about herself was that "I can't possibly do it well enough." Rather than being a person of no ambition, the lazy person is generally one whose ambitions are so exaggeratedly high that they are beyond reach. Abby, like other lazy children, said, "I can't live up to what they expect of me, so I just don't do anything." What she needed from her parents was less pressure and more encouragement. She needed to be accepted for herself, and praised for her minor accomplishments, rather than always being prodded to get busy and excel.

After I talked with Mr. and Mrs. Platt they began to see how much they expected of Abby, and how little encouragement she got when she did something commendable. Mr. Platt especially had been in the habit of reminding her that she could do better. He began to back away from his demands and to find ways to express his approval of her as she *is*. Abby showed the effects of his changed attitude at once, but it will take some time until she can reverse her laziness and become an achiever.

What if your own energy lags, and you find it difficult to respond to your youngsters in an appropriate manner? You need not feel guilty. A parent's loss of patience is usually tied into the parent's own expectations of his or her own behavior. If you expect to be the perfect parent, you're going to fail. When you feel exhausted and unable to cope, call a halt and allow yourself a breather. Only when you accept your own limitations can you help your child to accept his or her imperfections. Much of the frustration that parents experience comes from not knowing what to do with the child and feeling inadequate. Nobody expects you to be on top of everything all the time, so there's no reason to expect it of yourself.

Remember that a child needs a respite too. Just as it is not wise for a child to be continually inactive, neither is it reasonable to expect a child to be constantly on the move. Some children resort to laziness when they feel too much pressure from parents to be busy all the time with scheduled activities.

To become an achiever, your child's store of physical energy needs to be consistently high. It is true that many famous authors, inventors, and composers were frail and it is certainly possible for people to overcome their deficiencies. Alfred Adler was among the first to call attention to this when he wrote about organ inferiority and compensation for deficiencies. But the focus of this book is to help you, the parent, learn what you can do, as well as what the child has to do for himself or herself. Since you can't get inside the child to do his or her striving or growing, the most you can do is to provide the framework within which the youngster can best develop, grow, and perform.

8

The Pursuit of Learning

Academic achievement doesn't begin when a child enters school. It begins almost at birth as the infant prepares for life. From the earliest age, little ones soak up learning as they breathe. They want to know everything and learn to do everything; in short, to become as accomplished in the arts of life as everyone they see around them. The striving for significance begins then and continues throughout life.

The First Skills

At first they learn automatically. A parent meets the infant's total dependency for nurture and shelter and also shapes the atmosphere by supplying the stimulation of human companionship, conversation, and activity. The human contact along with sights and sounds are prerequisite to successful learning later. The foundation for academic success is laid in the early weeks and months of life as the baby learns by trial and error to distinguish one shape from another, one voice from another, and one texture from another. All the senses are used as the infant begins to organize the world around him.

As babies grow and make more and different demands on adults, their insistence sometimes becomes annoying. The interaction between the toddler and adults may determine whether the child continues to be eager to learn or turns off from education.

The toddler wants to know how to do it, and often too soon (in the adult's view) insists on doing it "myself." We need to watch, to listen, and to decide how much independence the youngster can handle, always being careful to allow maximum autonomy while protecting his or her physical safety. If you're uncertain whether a child can actually perform a task she or he wants to do, allow it, but stand by. Be available not to take over, but to answer a question or lend a hand if necessary, and then give your approval. Even if the task is not perfectly done, commend the action, the attempt, so that the child grows in confidence for the next time.

As the child acquires language, she or he may seem to become a nuisance with questions, sometimes following an adult around making the same query again and again. This may be natural curiosity bubbling up, but if it is repeated until the adult is annoyed, it is more likely to be the child's device to keep the adult busy with him or her. In that case, the appropriate action is to refrain from answering once you have responded in clear, simple language. It is better to rephrase the answer to assure that the child can understand the words used than to become increasingly annoyed as the child persists. Such annoyance escalates into scolding when an adult stretches patience too far. Stop trying to be patient when you begin to feel irritated; just smile and say nothing. Don't fall for the child's provocation. Better to risk being rude by not answering at all than to holler your response. Once you get into a shouting match with a child, you have entered a contest to see who is more powerful, and this will not contribute to the well-being of either of you.

However, remember that every child needs ample opportunities to explore, investigate, and try out new skills. Such opportunities abound in everyday family life, and the alert parent makes the time and the occasion for them.

A child observes the activities of the household during the first year, and as early as the third year may want to participate. When a toddler wants to help set the table, allow it. Of course you wouldn't let her or him handle your cherished breakables at that age, but your helper can easily put a napkin at each place, followed by a fork, a knife, and a spoon. Similarly, this young child can help clear the table under supervision. Helping to sort the laundry will not only give a child a feeling of participation, but help a very young one to learn to distinguish colors, textures, and shapes.

By assisting a preschooler in developing skills, you are preparing her or him for school, for work, and for life.

Don't be bound tight by the growth tables that appear in books for parents. They can be helpful, but one must remember that such tables are drawn from observations and are converted into scores from which mathematical averages are taken. An average is just a number that may or may not suit your specific, unique child.

For instance, the "average" child may not draw a recognizable shape until age four, but your child may show you one sooner—or later. The muscles are growing at individual rates and the child's performance is determined both by his or her mental and physical states.

My neighbor, Naomi, is not yet three. She speaks well,

but hasn't shown any special finger dexterity. However, when she received a gift of a small pair of blunt-tipped scissors, her mother, Mrs. Robinson, sat down on the floor with her to demonstrate how to use them. With a stack of construction paper, Mrs. Robinson first showed her daughter how to put her thumb and forefinger into the scissors' holes, then to spread them apart so that the scissors would open and then to bring the thumb and forefinger together so that the blades would cut.

It took about twenty minutes of alternately showing Naomi and handing the scissors to her so that she could try. Throughout, Mrs. Robinson spoke quietly and moved slowly but consistently. When Naomi made her first cut into paper after dozens of tries, she actually shouted, "I did it!" and continued for the next hour quietly practicing how to use the scissors, in effect teaching herself after the demonstration.

I can almost hear you say, "Now she'll cut everthing in the house," but my response is that just as she learned *how* to cut, she will learn *what* to cut. The competence Naomi feels in mastering the scissors far outweighs the risk Mrs. Robinson took in teaching her to cut. There are always opportunities like that for adults to help little children learn useful skills. True, Mrs. Robinson sacrificed time and patience, but one's own convenience often becomes secondary as we raise children. Everything we do together doesn't have to be scheduled in advance. A spontaneous lesson as described brings rewards beyond the accomplishment of the skill. When the other demands of life, work, and the family make it impossible for you to spend teaching time with a child, you can talk about it and let the child know about the situation. The days of a child's dependence diminish rapidly and it is necessary to provide for them.

A World of Resources

As soon as a child enters school, she or he becomes part of a group for learning, in contrast to the one parent/one child relationship of the earlier years. Whether the first school encounter is in nursery school, kindergarten, or first grade, the children will be sorted into groups. This is necessary in any school setting, where there are from four to thirty or more children under the care and leadership of one adult. The role of parents in the home then is to see the child always as a unique individual. The parents supplement the work of the school by relating directly to the child as an individual. However, at no time does the careful parent do the child's work for him or her. Although parents guide and teach, they must simultaneously convey to the child the message that school is the youngster's work, not the parents'.

The world is full of all kinds of information, much of it fascinating to the child. Parents or other adults can be most helpful in the learning process by introducing the child to resources. It is not a coincidence that the rooms in schools that used to be called libraries are now called "resource centers." For as the body of knowledge expands in our era, nobody can have all the answers and we need to know how and where to find them.

We continue to be partners in our children's search as long as they live with us. We introduce an infant to the world of learning by showing shapes, textures, and pictures. To prepare the very young child for the world of the printed word, it is essential that she or he have access to books and look through them in order to get the idea that words on pages have meaning, that pages are to be turned in order, and that ideas are communicated in other ways besides spoken language.

The grade school pupil needs our help in understanding the complexities of the larger world. It is especially important for the youngster to learn that although it seems that the whole world is on the television screen, there are many other worthwhile experiences outside, such as theater, sports, live music, and the many publicly supported places where one can go to be entertained and learn something too. Even in the absence of such institutions, there are botany lessons in parks, history lessons in old homes, and geography lessons in lakes and woods.

As the student matures, our assistance requires greater effort, but it is always assistance, for we can't do the learning for her or him.

You can't inject curiosity into a child, and make him or her want to do all these things; but the curiosity is there at the beginning, and it will flourish if it hasn't been quenched. How you answer a child's questions determines how her or his curiosity develops. You want to supply information, but that isn't always possible. What is possible is careful consideration of the way you answer questions.

Reply in such a way that the child's curiosity will stay alive, not be stunted, and increasingly the child will take responsibility for his or her own education. In the beginning, you show a child how to look up words in the dictionary, or topics in the encyclopedia, or find books in the library, but this becomes part of the youngster's own skills as she or he develops.

What if you are asked a question you can't answer? Many parents are afraid or ashamed to exhibit their own ignorance, and so they postpone an answer, or make an excuse, or come right out and say, "Don't bother me, I'm too busy."

Taking those conditions one at a time, don't be ashamed if you don't know all the answers. Hardly anyone does. Each of us comes to adult life with certain limited kinds of knowledge acquired along the way, and sometimes we get more, but usually only as we need it. Not the least of the knowledge we lack when we become parents is that training that would teach us how to be adequate parents. Well-intentioned, we flounder and wonder; but remember the courage to be imperfect.

When a child asks a question to which we don't know the answer, the best response is the honest one: "I don't know." Avoid turning the child away; offer to help find the answer. It doesn't have to be at that very minute, but the chances are that you can make a beginning in your response. It might be, "I don't know, but it must be in the encyclopedia. Take a look and tell me." If you don't own an encyclopedia, make a date to go to the library.

An encyclopedia is an expensive investment and one that is hard to keep current. But there are other reference works your home should have that cost much less. If you don't have a good recent dictionary, buy one. There are fine ones even in paperback editions. You might want to get one on the child's level to begin with, but have a complete one available so that the child can grow in ability to use it and understand.

Get an atlas or a globe or both so that you can help the child find the world outside the door. An almanac is another good resource for looking up facts.

If you and the child have exhausted all the reference books and the child is still interested, the search for answers may require a trip to a museum. If there is one near where you live, schedule a trip there. If there isn't one, or you can't get to it, it's appropriate to consider whether the child or you could find the elusive answer by writing to an authority. Often a local newspaper can be helpful in telling you where to direct your inquiry. You may have to make the telephone call or write the letter on behalf of a very small child, but use the occasion to demonstrate how it's done, and let the child do it if at all possible.

Don't be bashful about taking the child to the library to ask questions. Modern librarians receive training that goes far beyond the card catalog, and can be of unlimited help in finding information. Introduce your child early to the functions of the library so that he or she will feel at ease there, comfortable with the facilities and with the personnel. The time you spend there will pay dividends in the youngster's academic achievement.

Do you postpone answers to questions that stump you? Do you say "Not now, I'm busy"? That's not a bad thing to do, providing you really are busy, that you speak in a matter-of-fact tone of voice, and that you remember later that you put it off. The chance remains that when you're no longer busy and you offer to help, the child is no longer interested in that particular question. That isn't tragic. You have demonstrated your willingness, and there will be more questions at another time. The child will trust you and feel free to ask again.

But if you say "Don't bother me" or "Go away" you're damaging the very curiosity that must flourish in order for the child to become an achiever. You're saying "I don't want to help you: It's too much bother." If that really is your attitude, it's all right to speak the truth; but if you're reading this book, I assume you want to know how to encourage, not how to squelch.

Consider the foolish question. Your child might ask, "Why is it Wednesday today?" to which there really isn't an answer, especially if it happens to be Thursday. That kind of question doesn't mean that you are invited into research on the calendar; it may only mean "I want you to talk to me." There are millions of foolish questions, and sometimes the best way to deal with them is to give foolish answers, all in a spirit of fun. The child needs to know that an adult can engage in silliness, too. And on the serious side, many an invention or scientific discovery has come from a person who asked an improbable question.

Real Goals

In helping your child, beware of the "Utopia syndrome." That's pursuing the unattainable. In Adlerian terms, such a pursuit makes it impossible to realize the attainable. By stretching out to try to grasp perfection, you may miss the chance to catch the reasonable. As I said earlier, if we set the standards too high, we risk discouraging ourselves and our children from making the effort to reach what is reachable. Many parents pursue the unattainable, believing falsely that they can make sure that their children become superior. Their unrealistic demands are in themselves a deterrent to their children's development, and then they are likely to blame external factors rather than to question their own involvement.

The trouble with looking for Utopia is that you may miss the ordinary delights of life. Mrs. Silverman thought it was funny when she told me about her six-year-old son's vocational plans. He said, "Mommy, can I be a fireman when I grow up?" and she told him, "Of course, dear, as soon as you get your Ph.D." Now maybe that small child didn't know about the long years of study and hard work that lead to a Ph.D., but he did know that his mother was telling him his goal was too simple. She may or may not have been kidding him, but as in most kidding there was a large kernel of truth. If she were to persist in such expectations, she might disappoint herself and discourage her son. Almost every small child wants to be a fireman, and it's a respectable occupation. However, we all change our minds hundreds of times about what we want to do for a living, and that applies to adults as well as children. It makes no sense to eliminate from consideration the many kinds of work that offer satisfaction without academic prestige.

When asked, "What can a parent do to enhance the possibilities of academic achievement?" Ms. Tillie Hilfman, M.A., assistant professor of Early Childhood Education at Northeastern Illinois University in Chicago, answered as follows:

1. Give the child a good feeling about himself or herself.
2. Don't compare one child with another.
3. Neither be overanxious, pushy, protective, nor unconcerned, but find a middle way.
4. Listen carefully.

Asked to elaborate on her third point, she admitted that this is probably a most difficult attitude for a parent to establish, and commented further that a parent must avoid:

1. Preventing activity by overprotection.
2. Pushing activity on to the child.
3. An attitude of not caring.

Ms. Hilfman gave an example of a young man she knows who said of his mother, "If she hadn't pressured me all through school, I don't know if I would have my doctorate today, but I'm pretty sure I'd be a happier person. I continue to feel I'm under the pressure she put on me, and it hampers my life."

That reminded me of a man I knew, a highly successful composer, performer, and producer of jazz and commercial music. I asked him once how he became such a fine pianist and musician, and he responded, "My mother tied me to the piano bench when I was five years old and kept me there until I practiced long enough." He didn't complain about it, but I observed that he was then in his third marriage, his children had no respect for him, and his employees feared him. Perhaps if his mother had not used force on him he would have better personal relationships, and he might still have achieved musical success by his own doing.

These two examples happen to be both of sons and mothers, but parents push their daughters too, even more so lately with drives for equality between the sexes. Trying to liberate women, we must be wary of the imprisonment of our daughters as well as our sons by those Utopian expectations. All our children need encouragement and assistance in order that they may achieve their full potential as persons, not limited in any one sphere.

As an elementary teacher with many years in the classsroom, and now as a teacher of teachers, Ms. Hilfman is aware of the necessity for cooperation between parents and teachers. But she also knows of the rare teacher who can be a detriment to a child, and cautions that a parent must never be afraid to protect a child against an abusive teacher.

I would add that before you go to bat for your child against an abusive teacher, be sure you have good evidence of the suspected harm, because it is unlikely that you have observed it firsthand. Keep a diary or a log with a list of the incidents that make you suspicious, together with any pertinent examples of the child's work. Before you complain, look it all over carefully to make sure that your child is innocent in the situation. There are children who provoke teachers even more than they provoke parents, and you must try to see the teacher's viewpoint as well as your own and the child's, if you're going to be effective.

Samuel L. Woodard, Ed.D., professor of Educational Leadership at Howard University, Washington, D.C., has been conducting ongoing studies of children who rise from impoverished surroundings to become achievers. He discovered that it is indeed possible for children to overcome obstacles, and his research is directed toward finding out how they do it. From his work, he has distilled certain steps a parent can take to help a child succeed. His basic suggestion is that parents let the child know they are available for help if necessary. I would add that besides being available for help, a parent must communicate to the child in every way possible the parent's belief that the child can succeed. "I know you can do it" simply stated gives a child a powerful boost.

His guidelines for parents are directed toward enhancing the child's self-esteem, the child's individual competence (in tying shoes, for instance), the sense of family solidarity, and open communication. He too stresses the importance of the example set by the parents. What he has learned and recommends fits into basic Adlerian principles of child raising, and applies to all children, not just those from deprived backgrounds.

Academic Achievement

To understand the world of the child's classroom, we need to know what the school means by "underachiever" and "overachiever." Teachers assume that we all know what those terms mean, and so those labels are tossed around freely and a child may be destined to fulfill their intent.

I wasn't sure what educators mean by those terms, and I'd like to share my findings. The definitions that follow are excerpted from those in the *Encyclopedia of Education.**

> *Achievement test:* A standardized test used to assess knowledge and skill on any subject. An Achievement Quotient (AQ) is expressed as a percentile ratio of the achievement age to the chronological age.
>
> *Underachievement:* This is a term generally used to describe academic performance well below the expectations raised by the results of an intelligence test.
>
> *Overachievement:* This term usually refers to academic performance that is far better than one could predict from the results of an intelligence test.

Note that the use of these terms depends on the results of a test; without a test their meaning is lost. Remember that such tests are tools for educators. They are not infallible predictors of a child's future achievements. They are not foolproof, and teachers admit that. Ms. Hilfman gave the following examples of the use of tests before first grade, to determine reading readiness. She said she might tell a mother, "According to the results of our tests, your child

1. should be able to read with ease, or
2. is not ready for reading yet, or
3. would have a very difficult time reading."

* Edward Blishen, ed., (New York: Philosophical Library, 1970), p. 783.

None of these statements is hard and fast. Test results help school personnel to group children according to their needs so that each child can get the best possible instruction.

Ms. Hilfman commented further:

"Sometimes we would be wrong. Sometimes a child who tested low would go beyond the expectations of the test. That child would be called an overachiever. Assuming the test was right, we would say he was going above his capacity. On the other hand, a child who tested very high and didn't perform at that level would be called an underachiever. Other factors would have to be involved, and we would look into them.

"An achiever has something beyond intellectual capacity within him or her, some element of motivation that makes for success."

As you ponder how you can help your child reach academic success, don't overlook the experiences you can offer that are not directly connected to school. One of the best is the exercise in independence that a child gets by spending an occasional period of time away from home. It may be as simple as an afternoon with grandparents, or a "sleepover" at a friend's house, moving on toward an "overnighter" with day camp and then "sleepaway" camp from two weeks to ten. Investigate carefully before you trust your child to others, but don't deny the opportunities for increasing independence because you fear the child might be lonesome. Raising children is a long process of letting go, and a clinging parent doesn't help a child.

When planning family vacations, think about the kinds of enriching experiences your children might get along with the fishing, swimming, and sunning. If you're going to drive, make it a family project beforehand to plan the route you will take. You may find interesting places where you can break the trip with a stop that will be refreshing for everyone and informative too. Our family once became interested in cotton and how it gets from plant to fabric. On a trip through the South, we arranged to stop overnight in a small city in the cotton belt. An earlier inquiry to the Chamber of Commerce led us to a man who showed us around, demonstrated the machinery, and gave our son samples of products from the cotton boll that he brought back to his classroom. We still had time for a swim in the motel pool after our excursion, and that routine stopover became an event we all remember.

Academic achievement is dependent on many aspects of a child's life and personality, and there is no limit to the ways a parent can provide the kind of environment in which learning blossoms.

Teachers' Guideposts for Parents

Teachers have many specific suggestions for parents. They can tell you how to help a child succeed in school. Many of these helpful hints arise out of the common experience and wisdom of elementary school teachers. Lists of them circulate in schools, teachers' training colleges, and workshops for teachers. Those that follow were recommended to me. I call them "guideposts" because they point the direction in which parents can travel. I offer them to you as further illustration of helping your child succeed, especially in school.

- Accept the child as he or she is. Comparisons with other children are damaging.
- Be open to learning something from the child.
- Be open to suggestions from the child. Children have many good ideas.

- Don't be afraid to set limits and/or restrictions and then stand by them.
- Do not help the child to make any excuses.
- Encourage the child to feel that schoolwork is his or her own job for his or her own benefit.
- Encourage the child to wonder about things, to ask questions, to be curious.
- Emphasize the relationships of things: sorting and classifying, counting and measuring, exploring and creating.
- Expect children to take part in the work of the home by performing tasks regularly. When they have jobs to do at home, they can more easily understand the job of getting schoolwork finished on time.
- Follow through on any agreements you make with the teacher and/or the child.
- Give appropriate books and/or magazine subscriptions for birthdays, Christmas, etc.
- Give your children your time and respect.

Help your child to:
- Learn the names of things and people.
- See things in groups that are alike: all the big rocks, all the red beads, all the children.
- Recognize things seen before, to see how things are alike and how they are different.
- Notice changes in things: in people, toys, the room, or the buildings.
- Get acquainted with his immediate neighborhood.
- Develop a sense of responsibility by requiring the child to take care of a pet and/or her or his own belongings.
- Notice new words. Commend the proper use of them.
- Expand his or her vocabulary as you use an un-

familiar word in context. Don't "talk down" to a child.

- Learn to use the senses to smell, hear, see, taste, and touch, for this is the way people receive information.
- Learn that there is time; that there is past, now, and future.
- Learn to remember what happened a few minutes ago, yesterday, last summer.
- Learn to describe what is happening now and to speculate about what may happen.
- Let the child take responsibility for homework.

What else you can do:
- Make up stories together. One member of the family starts and others take turns adding to the story.
- Play spelling or math memory games—in the car, on the beach, anywhere.
- Provide a place for study and school assignments. It should be well lighted, away from TV and household traffic, with enough space for reasonable comfort.
- Provide a place to park school belongings. The children can put their books, completed assignments, gym clothes, and anything else they need in the same spot every night. Then don't remind them in the morning.
- Set an example by reading so that your children can see your pleasure in it. Read to them, let them read to you, and read together too.
- Take the time to listen to your child.
- Take your child to the library on a regular basis.
- Take family field trips. They can make history and other subjects come alive and increase a child's enjoyment of what is learned in school.

- Tell the child when you think she or he has thought a problem through well.
- Tell riddles, play with making up riddles.
- Tell the teacher about any change in the household, in the family, or in the child's routine so that she or he can be alert to any change in the child's attitude or behavior.
- Tell the teacher of your child's special interests and/or abilities.
- Watch what your children watch on television, and turn it off when it's inappropriate.
- When your child is unhappy about school, visit the teacher to try to find out why and what can be done about it.
- You and the teacher can be partners in the child's education. Ask the teacher how you can best make your contribution.

9
Fun and Games

All work and no play makes anyone dull.

Play is frolic—it ought to be fun, and the achiever needs it as much as anybody. It is a mistake to expect a youngster to outgrow the need for play, just as much as it is an error for an adult to concentrate on responsibilities to the exclusion of fun.

Having fun gives an individual a sense of joy and of exhilaration available from no other source. But much of what we call fun, especially for our children, does not produce joy, nor does it contribute to their sense of well-being or their self-esteem. Especially when we adults become overinvolved in the planning and directing of free time, we risk destroying the very enjoyment we're trying to provide. As much as possible, children should initiate their own good time.

The connection between play and achievement is that the person who plays better can work better. The child who gains self-confidence through play will carry that confidence over to his or her tasks. As a matter of fact, the tasks of life for very young children begin as play, as spontaneous free expression of the striving to learn. We watch them, but sometimes misinterpret. Then we intrude to organize their freedom into structured activities, in our zeal to be their guides.

Our mistakes occur when we schedule them into too full a program of classes, clubs, leagues, and activities. The emphasis should instead be on the creative activity stemming from within the child. All youngsters need opportunities for individual exploration so that they may taste of life's offerings and choose among them.

A story is told of the suburban child in a new community who read about boys his own age having fun climbing trees. He said to his mother, "It must be fun to climb a tree," and she immediately went to consult her local directory to see if she could find for him a class in tree climbing. It didn't occur to her that some things are best learned individually through practice, trial, and error. Of course, if there were no trees around big enough to support the boy's weight, she could merely agree that "Yes, it must be fun. You'll be able to try it when our trees get bigger."

The example of a tree climbing class may sound extreme, but it is too often true that children do not have the opportunity to learn informally, by their own choice. Parents, feeling inadequate, look for experts in everything, overlooking their own unique opportunities to help their children.

Not every random thought needs to lead to action, nor does every idea demand fruition. But it doesn't hurt to take a fresh look at what passes for play in the lives of our children and try to discover whether they are actually gaining in self-confidence, in social development, and in a feeling of self-worth as a result of those activities. The decisions we make on their behalf may mean a difference in results.

The Tools We Use

As I have said, we have most influence on the surroundings of the very young child. The atmosphere we provide and the tools (toys) we supply affect what the child does and how she or he learns. For a baby, play is a continual learning experience, and we can help to make it rich—not by going to the store to buy the packages marked with the child's age, but by watching to see what the child requires and helping him or her get it.

A tiny infant lying awake may find amusement in watching the beams of sunshine over the crib and will begin to distinguish shapes if there are some hanging within view. Thus learning begins.

As soon as the baby can sit up in a chair and hold something, she or he will delight in having a spoon to bang. Playing with empty egg cartons, butter boxes, or other packages in your kitchen will help a very young child discover how to open and shut them and what kind of sounds they make. When their use is over, they can be discarded and replaced without cost.

Instead of taking everything away from the path of the creeping infant, be helpful by putting something within his or her grasp that is bright and unbreakable. The trip by crawl then has a reward, and the child will feel successful and thus be interested in making further explorations. When the baby tries to grab something in order to stand, provide a chair with rungs if you can, so the little one can grab the lowest one first, working up to the erect position. Or maybe it's your leg that's handy. Don't pull away; stay there so that it becomes a support for the child's efforts to stand up.

A few drops of detergent in a pan of water will make

lots of bubbles for a toddler to splash in, and if there are some plastic dishes to be washed, that will combine the beginnings of work with fun. The objective of training a child to become an achiever is to help the youngster learn that work need not be drudgery, but that there is satisfaction in the performance of tasks as well as fun in playtime.

In order for play to be productive, it ought to require activity and imagination from the child. The trouble with television is not simply the quality of much of the material presented, but the fact that it leads to passive acceptance of whatever comes across. For the most part, television only inspires action towards buying; it gets the viewer involved mainly in the exhortation to go the store, or to get parents to go to the store.

Television is a cheap and handy baby-sitter, but the price is high in terms of what effect it may have on a child. If you want your child to develop discrimination in selecting programs, you will have to use discrimination in what *you* allow to be shown in your home. It may be a little harder to enforce careful selection, but it's worth doing. The time children spend just looking could be used much more constructively in active play or imaginative pursuits.

It is not true that a parent must always have an answer each time a child says, "But there's nothing to do!" Nor is it necessary to provide toys and constant amusement for the older child; it is not helpful for a parent to try to be a social director. For the adult to supply the ideas is to deprive the child of the opportunity to create them. The most helpful comment one can make to a child who complains thus is to say, "I'm sure you'll think of something." Instead, what often happens is that the parent exerts every effort to make suggestions, such as "Why don't you call up Johnnie to see if he'll come over and play?" or "Why don't you play with your new game?" The child seeks to place the responsibility for amusement upon the parent, and the gullible parent falls for it. The parent who wants to encourage the child will instead respond in such a way as to help the child make the effort; and the child who is allowed freedom of choice will soon invent activities.

There are many playthings that have the same effect as passive television watching. The dolls that do everything but breathe, for instance, leave little room for imagination on the part of the child. Looking at a wind-up toy as it goes through its motions is a temporary treat at best, but a music box that a child can wind up provides stimulation if the child is moved to respond to the music by dancing.

In contrast to the dolls that are almost alive, a cuddly toy can be imbued with unlimited attributes by the child who plays with it and may become a soothing companion as well.

Before you buy playthings, think about their purpose and use and whether they will actually contribute to the growth of your child's abilities and imagination. For instance, choosing "educational" toys for a child can bring frustration, for the puzzle that is marked for a four-year-old may be too easy for your toddler; or on the other hand, if it's too hard, it may engender a feeling of incompetence in the child who is not yet ready for it. There is great satisfaction in learning to master a puzzle, but there is also danger in overpowering a child with too many such challenges.

As a matter of fact, one of the universal complaints of parents as well as children involves keeping the child's room neat. What often happens is that children acquire so very many possessions through the generosity of parents, relatives, and friends, that it becomes almost impossible to keep them orderly. To test this theory, remove all the things that haven't been used in three months and see if the child misses them. Many parents have done so and discovered that their children are actually relieved when they have fewer possessions to monitor. Together you might decide to rotate certain toys, or to give them away. With fewer toys to take care of, a child's imagination will be called upon more often, and he or she will profit from the exercise of inventing ways to have a good time with minimum equipment.

If you do buy fewer toys, the money you save can be better spent on the reference books described in the preceding chapter and on games and equipment the whole family can share. A great source of fun is the family playtime in which the littlest members share without keeping score, and without regard for who wins.

Games Families Play

If you are convinced, as I am, that being a parent does not require being autocratic, you are already on the way to inventing games and pastimes you can enjoy with your children. It doesn't matter who has the germ of the idea. What is necessary is an emphasis on the joy of participating rather than on the drive to win.

With a big ball, gather around in a circle and pass it from hand to hand. Toss it lightly, trying to keep it off the ground and in the air. This means that the bigger people will have to be gentle with the littler ones because the joint purpose is to keep the ball up. You might make up a point system giving one point each time the ball falls, but it isn't a point for or against anyone; it's just the score of the group. You can set a limit of ten points for a game, and as everybody learns to play, the game may last longer and longer and be more fun.

Do you have a piece of rope long enough for everybody to get a handhold? Try a tug-of-war in which you start out trying to pull against each other on opposite sides, but when one side begins to give way, someone from the stronger side goes over to the weaker side, thus prolonging the fun. Rather than trying to overpower one another, you may find the game is over when you all fall down laughing.

Many people are concerned about the excessive emphasis on winning in our society and the effects it has on losers. Many new ways to play have been invented. They're available in books to help you get started, in ready-made games, and through organizations, all of which are listed at the end of this book.

Don't overlook sports such as running and swimming. Such activities can last all of a person's life, and are not dependent on organized teams or leagues for satisfaction. Any one person can engage in such activity alone, and the whole family can participate together. It isn't just an accident that running has become so popular in recent years. Joggers and runners have found great satisfaction in competing only against themselves, and at the same time developing their own bodies to a greater state of well-being.

Inside the house, play games with your children. Around a table, play a card game simple enough for the youngest—maybe even just matching colors, or, as the children get older, help them learn to play games they can master. They will have training in memorizing, in assessing other people's actions, and in making their own decisions, all the time having the enjoyment of playing together, enhancing the feeling of being an integral part of the family group.

It's of course gratifying for a child to win over an adult, but if the adult merely gives up, the whole purpose is lost. If the adult doesn't try, the fun isn't there. Similarly if a child is allowed to cheat, that younster may learn that cheating is acceptable, and may carry that over to other pursuits. Better to play a game the child can handle than to try to bend the rules to make winning possible. Better yet to find or invent new games so that you can have joy in cooperation rather than in competition. As partners rather than opponents, people compete against the limits of their own abilities instead of against each other.

There are sources for this kind of game, for many individuals and groups have begun to discover that fun arises out of cooperation even more than from competition. Moreover, people who work with children have also begun to question our society's intense preoccupation with winning. To obtain information about games your family can enjoy, consult the Sources and Resources list at the end of this book. It will lead you to new ideas.

There are other creative family pastimes. An old-fashioned one is the practice of reading aloud. It is not only valuable for one parent to read to one child. Reading gains new importance when a child reads to an adult who listens. It is tremendously constructive when every member of the family takes a turn. The family can decide together what the reading material is to be: fairy tales, poems, plays, stories, the Bible, the newspaper, or a book that interests everybody. Set aside a regular time for reading—possibly after a family meeting—during which each person takes a turn. A child who is learning to read may need help with difficult words, but the experience of reading while others listen will help that child gain the confidence to speak up in the classroom and in the world. Such confidence is a basic necessity for an achiever.

You can adapt such a process to other kinds of fun, too. Try sharing painting. With poster paints, finger paints, or watercolors, set out enough brushes and paint containers so that each person has a supply; then arrange sheets of paper around the table, one for each member of the family. Play some recorded music and set a timer for five minutes. Everybody starts to paint an individual picture when the music begins. When the timer rings, everybody stops and moves over one space, leaving his or her own painting in place, and begins to paint on the next sheet. By the time each person has gone around the table, every piece of paper has a joint painting on it. If some are better looking than others, each family member has a share in the pride, and no one feels inept.

The Spirit of Fun

A word of caution here: If adults or older children enter these activities with glum resignation, it would be better not to begin. There needs to be a spirit of adventure and anticipation for any of these games or activities to become fun. Parents have to shed their dignity, and even be silly once in a while, so that the atmosphere created can produce enjoyment for everyone. Otherwise it's just another chore, like doing the laundry.

You don't fool anybody if you fake it. You don't have to act as if family fun is the greatest invention since the Model T, but if you can adopt an air of experiment with a feeling of being open to chance, you may discover enjoyment that's fresh and new.

What about fun outside the family? Certainly children prosper from activities with their peers, and it is with them that they spend increasing amounts of time as they grow older. This is appropriate, and parents see ample evidence of the fun created among friends. But the growth of suburbia has produced a whole culture of organized activities in which the children are participants and parents the observers. We all know the eager parents who wouldn't miss a game. They form a regular cheering section each time teams meet. There's nothing wrong with having pride in the pitcher who throws a no-hitter. The trouble is that another child may sit on the bench throughout the whole game. Or the same great pitcher may be downcast another time when the team loses despite her or his best efforts. Organized play has grown to the point where there is too little opportunity for children to engage in unsupervised spontaneous pastimes.

The role of the parents in children's organized activities is questionable. Many parents enroll their children in organized sports, thinking not of the children's benefit but of their own dead dreams of excellence. The adults often hope, without realizing it, that their children will shine and bring glory upon mother and father. The resulting pressure—spoken or silent— on the child can take all the fun out of the sport. In such a situation, the parent views the youngster as an extension of himself or herself, and the youngster is thus deprived of the opportunity to learn to be a separate individual. It is not conducive to the development of a child's self-esteem to feel the constant burden of debt to parents.

It is far better for children to take part in a sport or activity of their own choosing on a casual basis, and let the parents stay home. That way the fun is much more likely to be spontaneous and the results much less crucial.

Better still, leave organized leagues to the adult professionals who make their living by their performance, and let children throw balls and swing bats and rackets for fun. Without the pressure to win, children may actually improve their prowess, thus increasing their enjoyment and their self-confidence too.

Classes in sports skills are fine, providing the emphasis is on learning for personal enjoyment rather than for competitive gain. Before you sign up your child, talk to the teachers to find out what the emphasis will be, and reserve to yourself the option of deciding whether it is healthy for your child's self-esteem. The same kind of caution is to be exerted whether the class is in crafts, drama, dance, or music. If a child has such outstanding talent that there is the possibility of a later profession, it is even more important that that talent be nurtured rather than diverted to be shown off.

The danger of exaggerated expectations lurks in making too big a fuss over a child's talent. Myra Davidson, who was an average student, showed talent in art when she was in junior high school. There was a local show in which some of her work appeared, and her father was naturally proud. In connection with the art show, a local newspaper ran a contest in which readers were asked to vote for the best painting. Myra's father spent hours on the phone asking everyone he knew to vote for Myra's painting. They did, and Myra won a blue ribbon.

However, when Myra later enrolled in college in an arts curriculum, her expectations of her own talent were so high that she could not meet them, and dropped out during her first year. She did have artistic talent, but its development was spoiled by too early exploitation.

If, after you investigate a class or a program, you decide not to enroll your child in it, you may err, but you may also save yourself much later anguish. In many families, elaborate plans are made, expensive outfits and equipment are bought, and the budget stretched because a parent wants a child to excel. Mr. Davidson, for instance, spent a lot of time and effort, thinking he was helping his daughter. But when a child senses the pressure of the parent's push, she or he may lose interest and courage, as Myra did, and become unable to live up to the expectations. Thus the way is paved for endless family arguments about the investment of time and money. It is similar with hobbies and clubs. They can be healthy and satisfying, especially if the child finds and wants them, but they can quickly lose their appeal to the youngster if parents overemphasize them.

While recognizing the need for the school-age child to have close companions in specialized groups, we want to be watchful of the kind of coercion that demands that they stay in troops and clubs when they have clearly lost interest. What seems like fun in the fall may pall by springtime, and parents have to be aware of the difference. When a child loses interest, if a parent persists in forcing a child to continue, the risk is that membership becomes an issue for conflict between parent and child rather than a source of pleasure for the child.

What if your child wants to join a club or group of which you disapprove? Examine your motives for disapproval first. There may be just a difference in taste, but if you are reasonably certain that such a group would be harmful or detrimental to your child, simply refuse to make membership possible. If enrollment requires an outlay of money beyond a child's allowance, or if it requires transportation provided by parents or service from parents, you can refuse. You may invite argument, but conflict is inevitable anyway. You can learn how to cope with such disagreements when everyone meets for a Family Council (as described in chapter 5).

As in other aspects of life, parents who want to raise achievers have to consider the welfare of the children and must govern their communications and actions according to the best interests of the child's self-esteem.

10
Children with Special Attributes

Each child is unique, with individual strengths and abilities. But some children have requirements out of the ordinary, often challenging parents to the outer limits of their imagination. These are the children whose particular gifts or deficiencies make them special. They may have unusual talent, extra intellectual ability, or, on the other hand, temporary or permanent handicaps. Such handicaps may be physical, mental, or any combination, together with normal functioning in other respects.

The practice, especially among educators and other professionals in related fields, has been to combine all such unusual children into a category called "exceptional." The emphasis has been mainly on compensating for the physical, mental, and emotional handicaps that exceptional children may have. Services to the exceptional child have concentrated on the handicapped child, and the result of recent federal legislation has led to the organized search to find such children so that they may receive the help they need. Less attention is paid to the subgroup called "gifted," largely because it has been widely believed that "they'll get along fine without any help."

One of my first experiences with the public grade school my children attended was to participate in a discussion with the principal and others about the appropriate grade to introduce cursive writing. The greatest concern expressed was for the children who might be forced to try to write before they were ready. Someone else asked about those children who might be ready to learn to write as soon as first grade, and the principal answered, "They'll do it without our help anyway." This remark is typical of the attitude toward the gifted or talented pupil. It is often assumed that the school need not expend extra effort on their education because they learn so quickly alone.

Another aspect of the disregard for children's varying rates of readiness was the very widely expressed command that parents not teach their children the alphabet or how to read before they enter school, for that would complicate the proper work of the teachers. Television programs such as "Sesame Street" have largely cancelled that dictum. Now our children are vastly more familiar with letters, words, shapes, and numbers than was earlier possible. We can no longer ignore the influence of the world on the education and development of very young children.

From television they learn at home in hours or days what formerly may have taken months of ordinary instruction. True, some of what they learn is not particularly to their advantage, but it is also true that the children who enter school today have had years of exposure to the world through the picture tube. This exposure complicates the task of the teacher as well as that of the parent.

Difficult as is the role of the parent in raising an "average" child to become an achiever, special responsibilities fall on the parent of an "exceptional" child. Such a parent needs not only to follow the pattern prescribed for all children, but also to exert extra effort in order for the exceptional child to reach her or his full potential. There are resources inside and outside your own community to help, but the basic requirement of these children, as of all other children, is the development of self-confidence and self-esteem so that they may reach whatever achievements their innate abilities allow.

The Gifted Child

Since less attention has been paid to the gifted or talented child, let us consider such a child first. Debra Kaufman, a young girl I know, is seven years old and in second grade at the neighborhood public school. She has been reading since she was four; writing down her ideas in a journal since she was five; and in the last year has begun to play the piano by ear, sometimes inventing her own variations on melodies she hears. She is now intrigued with gymnastics, learning the positions and movements and enjoying the physical activity immensely.

Debra is quiet in the classroom, but her teachers and the principal have become aware of her unusual achievements and feel that she should be removed from the neighborhood school to one that is better equipped to educate her. The Kaufmans are faced with an expensive dilemma: They recently purchased their home in an area known for its excellent schools; but the staff has recommended that Debra be enrolled in a private school many miles away. There is no one perfect answer to this dilemma, but the Kaufmans have begun to consult specialists in educating the gifted in order to make an informed decision. They have two other children, and although they want to provide the best possible education for Debra, there are limitations on what they can do.

Many children can do some one thing better than others their own age. When I speak of a "gifted" child, I mean the one whose ability is outstanding. Such a child presents a particular challenge to teachers as well as to parents. There may be more of them than we realize, for sometimes such a child will hide his or her talent in an effort to be just like everybody else.

Unlike Debra, who is quiet in the classroom, a gifted child may become a disruptive force, taxing the patience of any teacher. Such a child may turn his or her talents to disturbing others by wandering around the classroom, talking aloud out of turn, creating mischief, provoking other pupils, or any of many variations on inappropriate behavior. Such behavior can sometimes be traced to the fact that the assigned work is so easy that the child resists it. It becomes boring. Performing the exercises in a workbook designed to help a child become familiar with reading two-syllable words may be an utter waste for the child who already reads three- and four-syllable words with ease and understands the meaning of what he or she is reading.

Similarly with mathematical concepts. The child who almost intuitively understands the assigned problems may refuse to do the exercises that are supposed to lead to learning. A sixth-grade girl I knew complained about the level of her math class, saying, "I'm not learning anything new. It seems like every year it's just that the addition problems get longer and wider!"

The child who is disruptive in the classroom is a problem to the teacher, but the tragedy is that often these children are labeled "bad" or an equivalent, and their gifts go unnoticed and undeveloped.

In the home it may be just as hard to discover the gifted child's prowess, but the opportunities for observation are broader. A parent has fewer children to watch, for instance. And regardless of the number of hours a day a child spends at home compared to those spent in school, the family relationship is a closer, more continuous one, and there are different kinds of situations at home. Thus a parent can help a child to turn from destructive behavior to constructive activity so that his or her special talents can flourish.

The outstanding danger in raising a gifted child is to make a demonstration of the child. We have probably all been in homes where parents show off such youngsters. The gifted child is asked to recite a poem, read a book aloud, sing a song, or do any one of the "tricks" she or he has been taught so that adults may listen, admire, and applaud. The parents beam.

Such parents, Mr. and Mrs. Packer, came to consult me about their three-year-old, Kevin, who was becoming increasingly bratty and impossible to live with. Conversation with the family showed that Kevin has many special gifts. He speaks in full and complicated sentences; he enjoys doing puzzles; he plays checkers with his father and occasionally beats him; he can identify letters and numbers; and he is beginning to get the sense of reading. The trouble is that he can outsmart his mother, making it impossible for her to get along with him in the necessary activities of mealtime, playtime, and bedtime. She felt intimidated by his superior intellect, which he used to get his own way.

As the Packers describe their life with Kevin, it is evident that they are very proud of his abilities, and continually show him off to his grandparents, relatives, and friends. As a result, Kevin has acquired the mistaken notion that his significance in the world depends on his showing how smart he is. He does not enjoy the company of other children because he has been trained to hold center stage, to perform for adults rather than to be himself.

The Packers have a hard job ahead; they must encourage Kevin to continue to learn more and to use his superior intellect productively, while at the same time stop bragging about him. They also have to help him to learn to be with other children so that he can experience the give and take of normal living. He needs to be treated with the same kindness and firmness as any other child so that his special gifts do not distort his personality. Kevin's parents began by enrolling him in a nursery school, informing the head teacher of his particular needs, and since the arrival of an infant daughter they have begun to treat both children as people rather than as objects that exist solely for parental pride.

Since this book is primarily for parents, I won't presume to tell teachers and principals what they have to do with and for gifted children. But rather I urge parents to notice the special gifts and to exert extra effort to see that a talented child gets the kind of schoolwork that will be a challenge rather than a bore. Such a child also needs the kind of enriched experiences that the school may not be able to provide.

The Kaufmans, Debra's parents, have already discovered how crucial their relationship with the school personnel is. Unless parents can cooperate with the school, learn to understand what the school can do and what it cannot, there is danger that the child may become a battleground of the opposing forces: parents on one side, school on the other. The child, of course, would be the one to suffer. Parents must realize that the public school operates under laws and budgets, and can't put into practice all the innovations a parent might want. But parents may also discover endless suggestions and assistance from concerned teachers so that parents can supplement the work of the school.

For a gifted child, parents also have to search for extra learning opportunities. For this child even more than for the average child, there need to be encounters with libraries, museums, and other places of special interest. It is not enough to believe that a gifted child will find a way. Many of them do, but we have no idea how many gifted children are around masquerading as lazy or un-motivated. We see only those whose gifts are obvious.

The gifted child may even resist being so labeled. Norman Lang, a twelve-year-old I knew, had been tested at an early age and demonstrated abilities far beyond what was expected. He showed the promise of genius-level intellect, and was living up to that promise. In a con-versation with his parents over some disagreement, when he was reminded of that fact, he responded, "I don't want to be a genius. I just want to be an ordinary boy." For that statement there was no answer. Such a response from the boy indicates his reluctance to try to live up to his parents' expectations, and it is not unlike the characteristic responses of the so-called "underachiever." My point in mentioning it is that even the child with extremely high potential may resent the pressure of parents' expectations and feel inadequate to meet them.

Such a child may very early go far beyond the at-tainments of the parents in many ways. Norman's parents were intelligent people, but they could not understand the topics around which his ideas centered. Debra's parents' other two children have ordinary abilities, and the Kaufmans are really puzzled by her vast interests and accomplishments. It is no disgrace that your child knows more and can do more than you can. Your responsibility to her or him is still great. For the immigrant generation earlier in this century, it was taken for granted that their American children would surpass them; but in succeeding generations that point of view has been lost. It need not be. It's still quite all right for your children to go beyond your level of knowledge and attainment, and their ideas can become a source of enrichment for the entire family.

If you want your children to become achievers, the likely outcome is that they may reach a higher level of knowledge, of economic status, and of social prestige. But that doesn't make them better than you; there is no need to consider superiority and inferiority in your relationship with your children any more than with anybody else.

Help them to grow, be pleased about their attainments, but don't use them for your personal enhancement or feel inferior to them.

There is a new awareness in our society of the special needs of gifted children, and investigation will lead you to parents' groups as well as public and private agencies that are directly concerned with the requirements of the gifted child. Consult the Sources and Resources list at the end of this book for the names and addresses of groups that can help you. Keep in mind that groups of parents whose children have the same attributes as yours can be very effective sources of support.

You need outside help even when you first begin to wonder whether your child is in fact gifted. There are many tests administered by qualified professionals that help to measure the scope of a child's ability. Some of them can be administered as soon as the fourth year of life. As discussed in chapter 8, most schools use such standardized tests, administering them to the children in groups to assess the level of children's achievement. When you suspect your child is extratalented, however, an individual assessment may be more accurate. Such a test will help to plan the educational program for a child, and help a parent to know what kinds of enrichment will be most useful.

To find someone qualified to do this, begin at your local school to inquire if there is a school psychologist either on the staff or available for consultation. Also ask your pediatrician for a recommendation. If you still don't find an accessible person whom you feel you can trust, get in touch with the nearest university that has a department of education. There is very likely to be a qualified psychologist available through the university. When you do arrange to have your child tested, request aptitude as well as intelligence tests. Personality testing may also be recommended, depending on the individual child.

It may take a lot of searching to find a person who can evaluate your child and offer suggestions, but your child may have a great deal to contribute to the world through the development of special talents. It's worth the investment of your time and effort.

The Handicapped Child

Life also presents handicaps to our children, and such children need even more from us. In this respect, most states and school districts offer more in services to the handicapped than they do in services to the gifted. Get acquainted with the concept of the "exceptional child" and find out whether the needs of your child can be met. Do this as early as possible. Don't wait until the time of school enrollment to find out what is available, for certain handicaps are susceptible to very early diagnosis and treatment.

The handicapped child, as well as all the other children, needs the kind of experiences and interactions that will help him or her to have self-confidence and self-esteem. These limited children need optimal chances to grow despite their handicaps. The difference between the gifted special child and the handicapped one is that the potential of the gifted may go far beyond what one might expect, whereas the potential of the handicapped child usually carries noticeable limitations.

Another distinction is that while the parents of a gifted child may show off, the parents of a handicapped child may feel sorry for her or him, and this is particularly destructive. To feel sorry for someone is to give that person a message that you don't feel he or she can cope, which leads to feelings of inferiority and inadequacy that are an unnecessary burden for anyone. There may also be a temptation to protect a handicapped child more than is necessary, and this, too, is a disservice. One must have consideration for a handicapped person, while at the same time communicating a message that "you can do it" within the actual possibilities.

It is not my purpose here to list all the many types of handicaps a child may have, nor the many organizations and services that can help, but you need to know that federal legislation that recently went into effect spells out a national commitment to appropriate education for every handicapped child, including the most severely disabled. The impact of the laws enacted in the last few years has not been felt completely, and it is the responsibility of parents of a handicapped child to seek out and demand the required services and facilities. In addition, parents' right to participate in planning and monitoring their child's educational program is now protected by law.

To make sure that your child will receive an individualized education plan specific to his or her needs, exercise your legal right to participate in making such a plan. In addition, the school is required to get your informed consent before administering or undertaking any procedure with and for your child that is not routine for all children.

As with other children, a parent can be most effective in helping to create the kind of mental and emotional stability that will allow such a child to reach her or his full potential. As much as possible within the actual limits of the handicap, such a special child has to be encouraged to participate fully in family life and its tasks. There need be no apologies, but rather realistic recognition of the limits, with emphasis on the abilities. A crippled child, though confined to a wheelchair, can set the table or fold laundry; a blind child can answer the telephone; a deaf child can help with cooking and food preparation. There are many activities necessary to the smooth functioning of a household, and sharing in them will encourage the handicapped child to feel capable, despite his or her limitations. Never express feeling sorry for the handicapped child.

One major difference between being a parent of a child with special attributes, whether gifts or limitations, and being the parent of most other children, is in the parent's connection to the child's education and schoolwork. For most children, school is their business, and parents detach themselves from the performance of homework and similar responsibilities. For the special child, however, a parent must be investigative, informed, vigilant but not antagonistic, so that such a child is in a position to have the best possible opportunities. At no time, however, should a parent or any other adult do for a special child anything that such a child can do for himself or herself.

Admittedly, it's a very thin line that the parent of a special child walks: to seek and hopefully to find the opportunities for the child, but to step back and allow the child to use those opportunities independently. Basically, the pathway towards helping your child achieve leads in the same direction for all parents. For the parents of a special child the route is not quite as clearly marked or easily traveled.

Parents of the handicapped child can find much support and information through joining groups of parents with similar challenges. It is worth seeking others whose situations are similar to yours and starting a group if you can't find one.

11

Values: How They Affect Achievement

Everybody lives by his or her own values, whether or not we speak of them by that name. Some us talk of our "priorities" and sometimes we think in terms of "what it means to me."

Usually, when we speak of a value, we mean the monetary worth of something. Or if we put a value on something, we mean that we rate it in a scale of importance or usefulness, and generally we're still speaking of value in terms of money or its equivalent.

Sociologists, however, have carried this concept a step further to use the word *value* to mean the ideas, beliefs, attitudes, and assumptions we carry within us about what is good or important in life itself. As individuals we don't often question ourselves about our system of values. We take them for granted as part of the foundation on which all our perceptions and actions are built. We're not in the habit of trying to understand why we hold certain beliefs about what's important.

As a result of this, and a general vagueness about the subject of value systems, the concept of "values clarification" originated. Many people have become intrigued by this process of questions and introspection that helps one to discover what she or he actually does value. Such an examination leads to greater awareness and a clearer approach to life's decision making. You may want to seek values clarification sessions in your community. They are offered by local colleges, churches, and adult education institutes.

For a simple example of the abstract concept of values in connection with what we want out of life, let us think in terms of money, the commonest medium of exchange for value received. To put it in terms of merchandise will help to explain the differing emphases that different people have on what they value.

In a large store, there are many different kinds of merchandise available to us. Some of us may look particularly at cameras and shirts. There are several models of each, in different price ranges. If the price of a camera we want is more than we have available to spend at the time, we must make a choice. Some of the choices are these: to wait and save the money; to give up the idea of owning such a camera; to buy it on the installment plan; or to look for a similar one at a lower price. There may be other choices as well. Each person makes a choice on the basis of what he or she values.

But suppose I go to the store to buy a shirt that I really need. You're there too, also interested in the shirts. There is one shirt for ten dollars, basic and plain; one for fifteen dollars made from a more interesting fabric; and one for twenty-five dollars that has a distinctive cut and many additional features in the latest style. I might pick the fifteen-dollar one, you might choose the twenty-five-dollar shirt, and someone else the basic ten-dollar style.

Into the choice of the shirt goes the whole "value

system." It's not important to me to have all the latest features, because I need a shirt to wear to the office every day, and I'm practical in how I spend my money. You may be just as practical, but want the best-looking style because you're buying it to wear to a party. The third customer has exactly ten dollars put aside to buy a shirt, and so he buys the one for that price.

It's not too hard to figure out what to choose when we purchase tangible objects that bear price tags, but when it comes to making decisions in life, where the price is not so clearly marked, we face a much more difficult task. Our value system enters into every single decision that we make, whether we realize it or not. All of us need to become aware of what we truly value in life so that we can understand better how we actually make our decisions.

Since our children are absorbing their own value systems largely through observation of us and our influence on them, it is helpful to be clear about what we really value. For we cannot expect the young persons to adopt a value system we merely tell them about. We have to live it. They will decide what they value based on what they see and hear, and mostly what they experience. Through making their own decisions they will discover how the world works.

When we ourselves make decisions, we may sometimes make them in haste, sometimes recklessly, often in error. Or, on the contrary, we may agonize in indecision for so long that this becomes a decision itself, a decision not to do anything. Either extreme can spoil many opportunities in life and leave undesirable consequences.

Understanding our own value system is also complicated by our assumption that other people, especially those to whom we are close, have and cherish the same set of values as ours. But when we have strong disagreements with spouse, family, or friends, we discover that our value systems differ. The classic example is the disagreement between husband and wife over where to spend vacation time. He wants to go to the woods by a lake where he doesn't have to shave or dress up and can hike and fish. She'd rather go to the shore where she can soak up sun. Given a free period of time, each one wants to spend it in a different way, depending on what he and she separately value.

When there is also a child or children in the family, another dimension of disagreement is added. The children may prefer to go to an amusement park they've heard about, because they value the entertainment offered there.

How such conflicts may be settled has been discussed in chapter 5. The point of this discussion, however, is to remind you that such conflicts may relate to a difference in values. We all carry within us, within our lifestyles, ideas about ourselves, other people, and the world, and what we want out of life. At the foundation is our desire for, and striving towards, a feeling of being significant. We differ in how we perceive we can get that significance, that feeling of being important.

One person strives to make a lot of money; another reaches for fame regardless of money; and a third seeks the approval of other people. There are an infinite number of variations on individual personal goals, and all of them relate to the person's specific value system.

As I tell you how to help your children achieve, we assume that we all place a high value on achievement, however we define it. Other commonly held values in the United States are: individual effort, self-improvement, change, technology, movement, and physical comfort. We need only to look around us to see what importance is attached to these values, even though as individuals we do not rank them equally.

But it is essential to understand that our children may not automatically share our values and our aims. We generally assume that they will and find it difficult to understand when they don't. This becomes a severe problem in our relationships with adolescents and young adults, but it begins in childhood.

In a book about values, *Helping Your Child Learn Right from Wrong: A Guide to Values Clarification*, the authors, Dr. Sidney B. Simon and Sally W. Olds, say, "Most of the issues that concern us fit into the ten values-rich areas: family, self, friendship, society, morals and ethics, religion, leisure, money, work and school, and love and sexuality." The book is a collection of specific techniques by which family members can openly discuss their separate ideas about these concepts. It tells how parents and children can reach understanding of one another's points of view.

One thing is certain: Children adopt their own values as they grow, unknowingly absorbing them through their perceptions of others. The values they adopt will become incorporated into their manner of living according to their own lifestyle. They may include their parents' concepts or they may go in opposition, depending on the child's purposes and goals.

To set an example by living according to what you say you believe in and value is probably the very best way to influence your child. If you profess one set of beliefs but live and act in a contrary way, your children will see the contradiction and doubt you. If, however, your statements and your actions are consistent, your children are likely to observe your integrity, respect it, and adopt your viewpoints as their own.

Another aspect of the possibility that your children's values may be different from your own is that they are forming theirs in different times, under different conditions. Particularly regarding achievement, you may find that they are not as eager to "reach the top" as you would like them to be. The changes in our society over the past few decades have caused us to question many of the truths we thought were everlasting. Not too long ago the attainment of material goods and fame was considered to be the highest and best aim of all people, but today's young people question such goals.

At this moment it is impossible to predict the direction in which the pendulum of popular thought is swinging, let alone to predict where it will be when today's children are grown. Therefore it becomes urgent that children learn early to be as self-sufficient as possible, to learn how to make decisions, and to learn to examine their own beliefs in the context of the realities of the world.

Teaching Values

How can you help a child learn to make independent decisions? By offering every opportunity for choice as early as possible. The nursing infant decides when to stop sucking; that is an automatic choice, based on physical responses. The toddler may be given a choice of which toy to take along on a venture outside the home, but that choice should be very simple, between two or no more than three objects. When the youngster makes the choice, it is to be respected. If a parent says, "That's not the one," the decision is spoiled. Even if it seems a poor choice, the child has to discover that for herself or himself.

When a child begins school, she or he can pick out the clothes to wear and dress himself or herself. It makes no sense for mother or anyone else to make decisions that a child can make or to do anything that the child can do alone. Preliminary instruction in choosing and dressing may be necessary; but do it in a quiet time when there is no pressure to hurry.

Encouraging a child to make small decisions early is helping him or her to prepare for making decisions later, when the choices are harder and the pressure of peers may be great. Experience is clearly a good teacher, on a par with example.

As a child grows older, many other opportunities for making decisions present themselves. One of the most effective areas to learn about values and decision-making is in the use of money. Within the comfortable resources of the family, each child needs a regular allowance that he or she doesn't have to ask for. For a six-year-old, it can be as little as a dime a week, but it is the child's to spend, even foolishly. Parents must trust the child, assist only if asked, and respect the growing ability of the young person to learn what happens when the money is gone. For that reason no extra money is made available.

An older child, from about the age of thirteen, can become responsible for her or his own clothing wardrobe. Set up a clothing allowance that is reasonable for the family's income and standards, and help the child learn to choose and buy within its limits.

In connection with the use of money, the growing child learns how to communicate with salespersons, how to find an item he or she wants, how to use the telephone in a businesslike way, and in general how to act outside his immediate circle.

Throughout childhood, offer any opportunity you can to the child to make decisions so that when he or she leaves home there will be a background of experience in choosing, and deciding, and then in experiencing the consequences of those decisions.

The achiever will make many decisions during the course of education and training for adult life, and the child who has learned at home how to make them is much better able to cope with the complex decisions of life.

If you discover that the value system your child develops differs from your own, this does not mean that you have failed to instill a "proper" set of values. It may only mean that the child found other ideas and attitudes more attractive. Your responsibility does not extend to trying to change those values, even if you could, which is doubtful. The child is a separate person, and may find greater fulfillment in a direction that leads away from your ideas.

12

The Success Story:
The Achiever

How will you know if you have helped your child succeed, as the title of this book promises? You may never know, but consider these attributes of the person who copes successfuly with life. Such a person:

- Has self-confidence, self-respect, and self-esteem.
- Is independent and self-sufficient.
- Is capable of making decisions.
- Continues to learn throughout life.
- Never feels that it's too late.
- Is open to change.
- Is a realistic optimist.
- Is a cooperating, loving human being who contributes to the well-being of other people as well as himself or herself, in true social interest.

By "realistic optimist," I mean someone who sees the world and the people in it as they are instead of what they might be. He or she believes that humans, though imperfect, are valuable, and hopes to contribute to the welfare of other people besides himself or herself.

If your child trusts and respects others while still preserving her or his own sense of dignity and worth and has many of the above attributes, she or he will achieve those goals that are important to her or him. They may not be the identical goals you would have chosen, but then the purpose of raising children is not to fulfill your own ambitions but to help them reach their full potential.

You may measure success by other criteria, but there is no absolute measuring stick and it would be foolish to try to make one. Each person evaluates himself or herself according to his or her individual perceptions.

I've met and read about many people whom I consider to be achievers, and am especially interested in what they say about the role of their parents in their own lives.

Amy Morris, twenty-six, just graduated from medical school. Her husband, Ivan, recently completed his postgraduate medical training. I asked her how she happened to become a doctor, and she told me, "When I was about twelve, my father, who worked for the state Department of Health, told me I could become a physician if I wanted to. But I'd never known anybody who became a doctor, much less a girl who wanted marriage and a family. He used to clip articles out of newspapers and magazines and leave them for me to read, especially if they mentioned women physicians who were married and had children. He did that for about two years, and I didn't pay much attention to the articles. But then when I met Ivan, I was in college and he was starting medical school. He was the first person I ever met who actually did it, and I thought I could too. When we married, his experiences helped me see what I wanted to do."

Amy went on to say, "My father was right. I found the studies fascinating, and I'm really looking forward to completing my internship, having a family, and practicing medicine. It's been hard work, and it'll be harder, but I think it's worth doing."

Michael Christofer, a young playwright whose play *The Shadow Box* won both the Pulitzer Prize and the Tony award in 1977, was quoted in the Chicago *Sun-Times* on June 12, 1977, saying: "It's because of my parents that I have accomplished something. . . . I grew up in an atmosphere of love, affection and trust. I received a tremendous amount of support. They gave me the feeling I can accomplish anything and what surprises me about myself is that they were right."

These two young people confirm what Alfred Adler claimed, that "everyone can do everything." Lewis Way, in *Adler's Place in Psychology*, says, "There are very few persons, be they blind or paralysed, to whom there are not opportunities open for some outstanding compensation or at least a life of useful activity. Perhaps, therefore, a truer statement of Adler's position would be to say that 'Achievement is open to everyone.' "*

I too believe that everyone can become an achiever. We cannot predict the conditions of the world our children will live in as adults, nor can we predict how they will define achievement for themselves. We must prepare them for uncertainty. Ellen Goodman, nationally syndicated columnist, says the best way to prepare them is to "teach them how to think, about themselves and their lives and whatever work they plunge into, sidle in, or fall into."**

In order to do that, we have to help them also to develop their personalities so that they can become effective human beings.

---

* Lewis Way, *Adler's Place in Psychology*, p. 214.

** Ellen Goodman, "One-track job minds," Chicago *Sun-Times*, March 14, 1978, p. 38.

Maybe now that you're nearing the end of this book you're disappointed that I haven't given you more specific instructions on what to do and when to do it in order to guarantee that your children will become achievers.

Of course there isn't any guarantee. Why haven't I told you when to do what? Because nobody can figure that out better than you can. You're the one who knows your own child and can observe what she or he is doing and how the climate in the home, the school, and the outside affects her or him.

Naturally, we're all human, and we don't always know what moves to make. But here are some simple statements you can remember to help you when you're not quite sure what to do or say:

- Show, don't tell.
- Help, don't hinder.
- Inspire, don't preach.
- Encourage, don't squelch.
- Lead, don't push.
- Do what you can and don't feel guilty if you can't.

The most important aspect of your life with the child is the kind of relationship you have, the kind of bond you both build between you, for it is on the strength of that bond that the child blossoms.

I hope you've noticed the interchange of feminine and masculine pronouns throughout this book. That's my way of telling you that our daughters and our sons can achieve equally. Both girls and boys need encouragement, support, affection, and leadership from their parents. It no longer makes sense to direct our daughters only toward the traditional feminine occupations such as homemaking, teaching, and nursing, while the boys go into engineering, medicine, and administration. Each person, regardless of sex, deserves the opportunity to develop her or his talents and capabilities to the fullest possible extent, in whatever direction his or her interests lead.

13
Questions Parents Ask

All of us who are conscientious parents run into road-blocks from time to time. We can't figure out what to do next. We may read, study, think, and find answers to many of our common difficulties in raising our children, but then a situation erupts in which we feel inept. That's the time we want to ask another human being to look at the situation and offer a suggestion.

I've collected some of such questions parents ask and offer them here with my answers. Most of them refer to achievement, but it may seem that some of them do not. However, all refer to the relationship between parents and children, and thus affect achievement. Your questions may be different ones, but I hope that those which follow will be helpful to you too.

Question: Our son Gordon, fourteen years old, took his eight-year-old brother Adam to the park courts and began to teach him to play tennis. After a few weeks, a bystander spoke to me about Adam's natural ability. He wants to supervise his development as a tennis player, arranging for lessons with a professional to start immediately. He also says we should send him to tennis camp this summer, but we have other plans. However, we hate to deprive Adam of this chance if he really has such great natural ability. This man says he can make Adam into a top tennis player if we follow his advice. We don't know what to do.

Answer: If you follow this advice, you will be putting Adam into a narrow situation, concentrating his entire life around the development of a single skill. The pressure to excel would be heavy and possibly damaging. It is far more important that Adam be allowed to develop a wider range of skills in living as well as in athletics. If he has natural ability to play tennis, it is likely it extends to other sports as well. There will still be time to specialize.

Question: Sometimes my son Merrill, fourteen, gets an "A" in math, and then the next time a "C," or even a "D." Why doesn't he get "A"s all the time?

Answer: Maybe he doesn't understand all the math concepts being taught during the current term. A conversation with him on a friendly basis might disclose he is puzzled by some aspects of the course. Another cause might be that after he gets an "A" he stops doing the work and so is unprepared for the next test. To help him, ask for a conference with his math teacher, with his consent, preferably with all three of you present. Do not overlook the possibility that he is proving to you that he can't always live up to high expectations. If you are haranguing him about his grades, stop.

Question: My daughter Gina, twelve, comes home with an assignment from school and complains that it's too hard for her. When I offer to help, she says no. Then she continues to complain, and rarely finishes on time. How can I help her?

Answer: Gina may feel that she's not important to you unless she can get you involved in her schoolwork. It seems obvious that she doesn't want your help, only your worry. The best way to help her is to say, "I'm sure you wouldn't have this assignment unless you are capable of it. If there is any way I can help, let me know, but I'll trust you to do it." Say it pleasantly, don't say anything else, and remove yourself from any discussion of it. She needs to know that you truly believe she can do it.

Question: Every time my son Perry, nine, gets his report card he says the teacher is unfair. He tells me that all the other kids got higher grades just because the teacher likes them better. What can I do?

Answer: Perry knows how to play on your sympathies. You may be in the habit of feeling sorry for him any time he isn't on top. This is very damaging to his own sense of worth. Assume that the teacher is fair, but on the outside chance that there may be a basis for his complaints, ask her at a conference if Perry really does get lower grades than all the others, and ask her to tell you why.

Meanwhile, examine your own attitude toward Perry and see if he could be using this complaint to arouse your concern. He may be displaying inadequacy for a purpose.

Question: My husband's family are all musicians, and our daughter Paula, seven, shows clear signs of natural talent. She plays the piano by ear, but refuses to discipline herself to practice. How can I make her take music more seriously?

Answer: Paula may feel too much pressure from the family to become a musician. Whatever the reason, you cannot make her take music more seriously any more than you can enforce effective practice. Allow her to continue to play by ear, discontinuing piano lessons if necessary.

She may want to start again if she feels the pressure is off. Examine your relationship with her in general, and try to find out whether she has another purpose in resisting your wish that she practice. Sometimes children choose our most vulnerable dreams to resist because they sense how great will be our disappointment.

Question: My daughter Nicole, eleven, wants to preserve her privacy by keeping us out of her room. She shuts the door and says she's doing homework, but I'm not sure. Don't I have a right to see what's going on in there so I can make certain she's really studying?

Answer: Nicole is entitled both to privacy and to control of her own homework. She needs to learn to study without anyone prodding her, and so it's really better if she closes the door. Everyone in the family is entitled to privacy—children as well as parents.

Question: What can I say to my son Bradley, nine, when he comes home dejected because he didn't get an "A"?

Answer: You have to assure him that he's still okay with you. If you feel sorry for him you send him the message that he can't cope; that he's too small, too vulnerable to face reality. That will only make him feel worse. Listen to him if he wants to talk. A casual remark like "That doesn't make you bad" can change the teary countenance to a smile on his face, providing you smile warmly as you say it and really mean it.

Question: My daughter Fern, eleven, is successful in almost everything she tries, but occasionally she's passed over for an honor, and she's crushed. What can I say to help her?

Answer: If she already has the idea she must excel in

order to be worthwhile, it won't help to argue with her. You have to cultivate an attitude that separates her deeds from her self. Let her know she hasn't lost your love or your approval. This means making less fuss over her triumphs so she can make less of her losses. When she learns that her worth does not depend on how many honors she earns, she will be less hurt when one eludes her.

Question: Our three children are all good students, but they complain that their classmates get as much as five dollars for every "A" and we don't pay anything. Will it encourage them to give them money when they bring home high marks?

Answer: If you pay for high grades, you teach your children bribery. You communicate the message that a person need only do something for a reward. The family's value system can be explained in a discussion about this subject. You cannot control what other parents do for their children, but you can decide for yourself what *your* standards are. To pay for a grade is to teach a child to perform only for payment rather than from inner conviction. Don't do it.

Question: If a child announces an idea that's preposterous or dumb or dangerous, how can we refuse? Or should we give our consent?

Answer: Let the child express any idea. Listen, but neither argue nor agree. If the performance of the idea would be dangerous, your responsibility is to prevent it; but if it would merely be innocuous, let it happen. The child will find out whether or not it was "dumb." Remember that you control your own participation, and can refuse to help the child carry out the idea if you believe it to be inappropriate.

Question: Should we read to our children from mythology books and the classics while they are still young, before these books become required reading? That might give them a head start, but we're not sure if such material would be right for young children.

Answer: Reading aloud is no fun if it's a "should." Let your choice of what you read depend on whether you enjoy reading it and the children enjoy listening. Otherwise, it's just one more annoyance to which they have to submit.

You may not even like to read aloud. I never did. I didn't read to my own children, but that didn't stop them from eagerly learning to read; in fact, it may have made them more eager to learn to read for themselves. It's very difficult to do something you don't enjoy and make it fun for the others. When and if you read to your children, choose material that you like, and judge its suitability by the children's response.

Question: Are the so-called "educational" toys really helpful?

Answer: They can be, but ordinary playthings (as described in chapter 9) can be far more instructive. The trouble with educational toys is that they can stifle the creative process. The best toys are those that challenge the imagination and ingenuity of a child, and these are often the simplest.

Question: Our daughter Ingrid, ten, puts on an act of having a headache or coming down with a cold whenever we have guests. She interrupts whatever we're doing to get our attention. If we don't immediately respond, our guests think we are poor parents. How can we handle this?

Answer: Make sure before company comes that Ingrid

is not actually sick. Then ignore her completely, telling your guests what you are doing and why. Take her by the hand to her room, if she persists, and tell her it is an adult party. You do take the risk that your guests will disapprove, but sometimes that is the price to be paid. It would be helpful if you would make sure that Ingrid gets enough attention from you at other times when she is not annoying you. Invite her to help prepare for the arrival of the guests next time so that she does not feel totally excluded.

Question: People say that children should be allowed to ask questions and explore their environment, to help them learn. But I want my children to be polite and well behaved. How can they do both?

Answer: Teach your children to be polite in the way they ask questions, and to respect the rights of others when they explore the environment. Begin in the privacy of the family teaching and showing respect for each other. One of the ways to help them learn how to behave outside the family is to rehearse the kinds of interactions they will have as you act out the roles of other people. If the way they ask questions seems disrespectful or inappropriate, under rehearsal conditions you can discuss the correct way, and point out why it's important to be courteous and considerate of others.

Question: I know that we shouldn't put pressure on our son Gideon. He's twelve, showing the signs of early adolescence, and struggling to get along in a new junior high school. He does his schoolwork, but my wife nags him to do better all the time. Nothing I tell her makes her stop. What can I do for Gideon?

Answer: The first thing you can do is stop quarreling with your wife about him, since it doesn't seem to be doing any good. The best thing you can do for Gideon is to spend some time with him alone so that he learns that you value him as he is, without mention of what he ought to be doing. He has undoubtedly formed his own ideas of how to cope with his mother, and has realized that your expectations of him are different. When you do spend time with him, let him choose what you do together so that you both can enjoy it.

Question: I'm a single parent, divorced and not remarried. I work full time and I'm trying to raise Norris, ten, and Portia, eight. Their father lives out of state and is no help to me at all. What can I do to help them with my very limited time and resources?

Answer: Under these circumstances, the best thing you can do for them is to allow then to operate the household to the limits of their ability. If you teach them the necessary tasks and trust them to do them, they will feel an increased sense of responsibility for themselves and for the family unit, together with an expanded feeling of confidence. This will at the same time lessen the demands on you so that you will have fruitful time to spend with them rather than struggling to keep up with the household chores. There are only a few home chores that children this age cannot perform succesfully; those you can all do together. Try to cultivate with them a sense of total cooperation among the three of you in a difficult situation. This will help them each to feel important.

Question: Our children are both in their early teens, and fond of contradicting us by telling us about "all the other kids." Usually, "all the other kids" can stay out later, or have the car more often, or have other privileges we don't grant. How can we influence our children in the face of so much peer pressure?

Answer: Peer pressure is real. It exists and influences our children of all ages. However, this is no reason for a parent to surrender. The child who is respected at home and accepts the family values is more likely to resist the pressure of others to engage in unlawful or undesirable behavior. In matters of taste, such as dress, allow freedom of choice. The pitfall for parents is that they are afraid to uphold their own principles for fear of community disapproval. The chances are that other parents are just waiting for someone to hold the line against what "all the other kids" are saying or doing

Question: Our children all compete with one another. If one gets an "A," she lords it over the others. The one who gets a lower grade makes many excuses. The third one is an athletic star who shows off his trophies. We try to tell them not to fight and we try to treat them all the same, but nothing we do seems to stop the squabbling. How can we handle their competition and their demands on us?

Answer: The only way to handle competition among siblings is to ignore it completely, to remove yourself from its demands. The general purpose of fighting among sisters and brothers is to get a parent or parents involved in trying to mediate. As long as a parent is willing to be the judge, the children are willing to continue to quarrel. You have to inform them that their differences are their own business and that you will let them handle them. Then stay out of it, even if it means going to another room and shutting the door.

Question: How can we recognize when our child has a problem?

Answer: When you have open communication with your child, she or he will tell you when something is bothering her or him. If you don't have open communication, you already have a problem. The difficulty often comes in deciding whether there is a problem serious enough to seek help. If it's causing you concern, look to a parent education group, a school counselor, or another qualified professional with whom to discuss it. Often just talking about it directly clarifies it for you so you know how to proceed.

Question: Sometimes, despite all my best efforts I get discouraged raising my children. So often what I do or say turns out wrong, and I don't know how to make it right. Where can I turn then?

Answer: You have the normal doubts of a concerned parent. A group of other parents in a similar situation can be a source of support and assistance to you. You can all study together and learn what to expect and what to do about it. If there is no such group in your community, start one. You can find other parents in the same boat through the school your children attend, your church, a community organization, or by placing a note on a supermarket bulletin board.

Consult the reading list at the end of this book. Begin with one article or one book that interests you, with as few as three other parents. In the Sources and Resources list you will find associations to whom you can look for guidance. Members of the North American Society of Adlerian Psychology have specific experience in such groups. Write to them. Get started so you can help yourself and your child.

Sources
and Resources

The following sources offer information and various aids for parents interested in helping their children along. Write to these places explaining what questions you have or the services you seek.

GAMES

Family Pastimes
Jim Deacove
R.R. #4
Perth, Ontario
Canada K7H 3C6

New Games Foundation
PO Box 7901
San Francisco, California 94120

The Ungame Co.
1440 South State College Boulevard
Building 2 D
Anaheim, California 92806

PARENT EDUCATION

Family Education Division
North American Society of Adlerian Psychology
159 North Dearborn Street
Chicago, Illinois 60601

GIFTED CHILDREN

National Association for Gifted Children
217 Gregory Drive
Hot Springs, Arkansas 71901

Office of Gifted and Talented
U.S. Office of Education
Donohoe Building
Room 3835, 400 Sixth Street, SW
Washington, D.C. 20202

GIFTED AND HANDICAPPED CHILDREN

Council for Exceptional Children
1920 Association Drive
Reston, Virginia 22091

HANDICAPPED CHILDREN

"Closer Look"
National Information Center for the Handicapped
PO Box 1492
Washington, D.C. 20013

TEACHING AIDS

Schoolmasters Teaching Aids
745 State Circle
Ann Arbor, Michigan 48104

TOYS FROM CASTOFFS

U.S. Department of Health, Education & Welfare
Office of Human Development
Washington, D.C. 20201
(Pamphlet: "Beautiful Junk"
DHEW Publication No. OHD 76–31036)

Suggested Reading

Adler, Alfred. *The Science of Living*. Garden City, N.Y.: Doubleday Anchor Books, 1969.

———.*What Life Should Mean to You*. New York: G. P. Putnam's Sons, 1958.

———. *The Education of Children*. Chicago: Henry Regnery, 1970.

Beecher, William and Beecher, Marguerite. *Beyond Success and Failure*. New York: Julian Press, 1966.

Briggs, Dorothy Corkille. *Your Child's Self-Esteem*. Garden City, N.Y.: Doubleday & Co., 1970.

Corsini, Raymond J. and Painter, Genevieve. *The Practical Parent: ABC's of Child Discipline*. New York: Harper & Row, 1975.

Daly, Margaret. "All Those Tests Your Children Take and What They Really Mean." *Better Homes and Gardens*, Vol. 55, no. 10, October 1977.

Dinkmeyer, Don and Dreikurs, Rudolf. *Encouraging Children to Learn: The Encouragement Process*. Englewood Cliffs, N.J.: Prentice-Hall, 1963.

———— and McKay, Gary. *Raising a Responsible Child.* New York: Simon and Schuster, 1973.

Dreikurs, Rudolf. *Children: The Challenge.* New York: Hawthorn Books, 1964.

————. *Psychology in the Classroom.* New York: Harper & Bros., 1957.

————, Gould, Shirley, and Corsini, Raymond J. *Family Council.* Chicago: Henry Regnery, 1974.

————, Grunwald, Bernice B., and Pepper, Floy C. *Maintaining Sanity in the Classroom.* New York: Harper & Row, 1971.

Dunn, Rita and Dunn, Kenneth. *How to Raise Independent and Professionally Successful Daughters.* Englewood Cliffs, N.J.: Prentice-Hall, 1977.

Fluegelman, Andrew, ed. *The New Games Book.* Garden City, N.Y.: Doubleday & Co., 1976.

Gould, Shirley. *Teenagers: The Continuing Challenge.* New York: Hawthorn Books, 1977.

Kalb, Jonah and Viscott, David. *What Every Kid Should Know.* Boston: Houghton Mifflin, 1976.

Maeroff, Gene I. "The Unfavored Gifted Few." *New York Times Magazine.* August 21, 1977.

McNamara, Bernard and McNamara, Joan. *The Special Child Handbook.* New York: Hawthorn Books, 1977.

Painter, Genevieve. *Teach Your Baby.* New York: Simon and Schuster, 1971.

Schwartz, Sheila. "The Adolescent and Human Values." *The Humanist,* July/ August 1977.

Simon, Sidney B. and Olds, Sally W. *Helping Your Child Learn Right from Wrong.* New York: Simon and Schuster, 1976.

Sisk, Dorothy A. "What if Your Child is Gifted?"

American Education, Vol. 13, no. 8, October 1977. (Available as free pamphlet from Consumer Information Center, Pueblo, Colorado 81009.)

Way, Lewis. *Adler's Place in Psychology.* New York: Collier Books, 1962.

Woodard, Samuel L. "Ten Ways to Help Your Child Succeed." *Ebony,* Vol. 32, no. 12, October 1977.

Index